PIZZA ON THE GRILL

100+ FEISTY FIRE-ROASTED RECIPES FOR PIZZA & MORE

EXPANDED

Elizabeth Karmel & Bob Blumer

The Taunton Press

 **The Taunton Press**
Inspiration for hands-on living®

The Taunton Press, Inc., 63 South Main Street, PO Box 5506, Newtown, CT 06470-5506
e-mail: tp@taunton.com

Editor: Carolyn Mandarano
Copy editor: Nina Rynd Whitnah
Indexer: Heidi Blough
Jacket/Cover design: Michael Amaditz
Interior design: Michael Amaditz
Layout: Cathy Cassidy & Lynne Phillips
Illustrator: Christine Erikson
Photographers: Matt Armendariz & Christopher Hirsheimer
Front cover photographer: Christopher Hirsheimer; Back cover photographers: Christopher Hirsheimer (left
   and right), Matt Armendariz (center)
Food & prop stylist: Melissa Hamilton, except for pp. 8, 13, 15, 25, 26, 32, 34, 41, 47,
   82, 101, 115, 128, 132, 138, 155: Bob Blumer & Elizabeth Karmel, with assistance
   from Alexis Hartman

Library of Congress Cataloging-in-Publication Data

Karmel, Elizabeth.
  Pizza on the grill : 100+ feisty fire-roasted recipes for pizza & more / Elizabeth Karmel and Bob Blumer.
     pages cm
  Includes index.
  ISBN 978-1-60085-828-4 (paperback)
1. Pizza. 2. Barbecuing. I. Blumer, Bob. II. Title.

TX770.P58K37 2014
641.82'48--dc23

Printed in the United States of America
10 9 8 7 6 5 4 3 2 1

To the wines and winemakers that inspired us as we wrote this book. And to KCRW.com, the eclectic Internet radio station that kept us hummin' along as we wrote this book in New York City, Chicago, and Los Angeles.

ACKNOWLEDGMENTS

First, a global thank you to everyone who helped us write, form, and massage this labor of love. Before there is a book, there is an agent, and Alfred Geller did a heroic job of representing us as a team. Kirsten Newman-Teissier and Rose White are the foundation of the operation, and we couldn't have written the book without either of them. Elizabeth's sister Mary Pat tested the dough recipes and lent us her children so we could prove that even toddlers can make their own pizza.

We tested all the recipes with the help of two crackerjack culinary grads, Lynndy Ackerman and Tanisha D'Antignac, and our master taste tester and mood elevator, Kate Zankowicz. Special thanks to David "the crust you can trust" Sanfield for the 150 balls of divine dough he provided from his awesome restaurant, Pitfire Pizza. More thanks go to Susie Bynum, Sarah Powers, St. Francis®, Domaine Carneros®, Sequoia Grove®, and other treats from Kobrand; thanks to Wilson Daniels for educating us on other-worldly wines; we toast Paige Poulos, Joel Quigley, and all the wonderful wineries they represent including the fabulous Murietta's Well and Imagery; and finally thank you to our good friend and fellow grilled-pizza fanatic Mary B. Burnham for the Geyser Peak® Block Collection.

Many thanks to Pam Hoenig for championing the concept and for the many fine folks who rallied to make this a great book—our wise and unflappable editor Carolyn Mandarano, the omnipresent Maria Taylor, the supportive Susan Edelman, tastemaker Carol Singer, publisher Don Linn, and friend Susie Middleton. The gorgeous photographs are courtesy of the fine eye and hand of Christopher Hirsheimer and Melissa Hamilton. Huge thanks to Robert Laub and all our friends at Harold Import Company—distributor of Elizabeth's Grill Friends™ and Kitchen Friends™ lines. Thanks to Mark Kelly and Bob Kellerman of Lodge Manufacturing® for a foundry of cast iron and the key to making perfect grilled pizza on a charcoal grill, the Cast Iron "Pizza" Grill Pan and the beautiful red cocottes. Many thanks to Jeanine Thompson and Weber-Stephen Products Company for the great grills with all the bells and whistles that they lent us for the photo shoot.

Thanks to Julia Stambules for representing so many of our favorites so well! Thank you on behalf of Wusthof®, Microplane®, Leiftheit, and Meyer®. Rachel Litner, we can't make a chimichurri without thinking of you and Waring®, or dough without thinking of you and Cuisinart®. Mike Staib and Ergo Chef® make a knife perfect for ergonomically minded chefs and home cooks. Our pizzas popped from the beautiful wood cutting boards and special surfaces provided by Candice Gohn and J. K. Adams Company and Susan Jardin and Emile Henri. Exotic mushrooms and produce arrived overnight from Robert Schueller and Melissa's Produce, and the pulled pork was expertly smoked by Melissa Hamilton's friend Hugh Mangum, maker of Mighty Quinn Barbecue Sauce.

Finally, a special note of gratitude goes to the following folks for their unconditional support of whatever project we may be working on: Elizabeth's father, Big Lou, and her mother, Lynn, who gets called on for the answers to all kinds of obscure cooking questions. Bob's friend and business manager Norman Perry, Sage-at-large Karl Wachter, John Lineweaver, Elizabeth's cousin on the Odom side and designer extraordinaire; Gretchen and Jeff Belmonti, Nat Teissier, Marian Temesvary, Richard Ruben, Rick Smilow and the rest of the team at ICE in NYC where Elizabeth teaches, Sharon Franke, Amy Tunnicliffe, Pete Savely, and John Kuhlmann; Marc Glosserman, John Shaw, and Sarah Abell from Hill Country. The home front was kept clean and calm by Teresa, Eva, Murray, and Perkins. And finally, all those wonderful folks (Surreal Gourmands everywhere, members of the GATG LadyBug Club, students, and consumers) who buy our books and products and allow us to do what we have so much fun doing—in this case grilling pizza for a living!

Further Acknowledgements for *Pizza on the Grill Expanded edition*

Likewise, this revision could not have been completed without support from many of our culinary friends—old and new. We met Matt Armendariz the day before our shoot and instantly fell in love with his demeanor and his special photographer's eye! All of the new shots in the book are courtesy of him and his expert staff. The gluten-free dough puzzle was a big one, and we couldn't have solved it without the assistance of the meticulous Kara Mickelson. A special shout-out to new friends from Revol, Tenaya Da Silva and Anne Valette, who provided us with beautiful culinary porcelain with which to stage our photos, and Larry and Luanne from The Perfect Peel in Appleton, Wisconsin, for making the stunning handmade pizza peels with the title of our book etched on them. Big thanks to Jennifer Lally and all of Elizabeth's friends at Nespresso℠ for keeping us happy and caffeinated with the petit but powerful Pixie Nespresso machine. Old friends and unconditional supporters always at the ready to help with any photo shoot include especially the following folks: Jeanine Thompson, Brooke Jones, and Mike Kempster, Sr., from Weber-Stephen Products Company; we couldn't grill pizzas without them! Lisa Callaghan from All-Clad® helped outfit our kitchen, and Dan Kulp and Rachel Litner came through with Epicurean cutting boards and peels. Julia Stambules once again rounded out what we needed with Meyer cookie sheets, Wusthof knives, and lots of Microplane graters. We appreciate each and every one of you and wouldn't have these gorgeous new photos without your help and your products!

CONTENTS

INTRODUCTION
from first edition

Welcome to the church of grilled pizza. If you think that's a joke, we aren't kidding. Once you start making grilled pizza, it'll be like "getting" religion. You'll want to preach the word to everyone. Fanatics that we are, we worship the heavenly crust as frequently as possible.

The two of us met ten years ago at a BBQ industry event and bonded over grilled pizza. We went on to discover that our mutual love centered on the crunchy, slightly smoky crust of grilled pizza. After returning to our respective cities, we couldn't stop talking pizza—we were driven to take it to the next level. After countless hours on the phone and months of experimentation, we finally had our epiphany. The secret to the perfect grilled pizza was a perfect crust. And it's not always about the recipe for the dough (although great dough does make a difference you can taste); it's about how the dough is cooked. By using a combination of direct and indirect heat, we achieved a perfectly crisp, golden brown, crunchy, smoky crust each and every time. (We call this proprietary method our 1-2-3 Technique.) From there we went on to gild the lily with our own combinations of non-traditional toppings and funky cheeses. We were hooked! Ten years and a squillion pizzas later, we have decided that it is time to share the love (and our favorite recipes) with you.

In addition to our crust, there is another thing that distinguishes our pizzas from the everyday pie. We do whatever it takes to infuse maximum flavor into each of the components that make the pizza—like our sauces and toppings. The resulting layers of flavor make our pizzas—like the pizzas in gourmet restaurants—taste so much better than those from your average pizzeria. Not only do we use the heat of the grill to caramelize the crust, but we grill many of our ingredients to maximize their flavor before they become toppings.

Beyond the life-changing flavor and texture of grilled pizza, part of what attracted us to this delectable and versatile food in the first place is that it takes such little effort and so few tools for such a huge reward. You don't need any fancy-schmancy gear or garb to enjoy the divine pleasures of grilled pizza. In fact, all it takes to get started is a backyard grill. We absolutely, positively *guarantee* that, with your grill and our 1-2-3 Technique, you will be hooked—but we can't take responsibility for your addiction!

And don't worry, we promise you that if you follow our steps your crust will not slip between the grates, nor will it burn like hellfire and damnation. All say Hallelujah!

—2007

WE'VE BEEN REBORN!

A lot has changed since the first edition of this book was released. America has become more food conscious and culinarily adventurous. And recipes that were once considered intimidating are now viewed as a fun way to decompress after a hard day's work. In the food categories nearest to our hearts, year-round grilling has continued to gain in popularity, and pizza has become so ubiquitous that Americans practically think they invented it.

Diets have changed, too. In particular, a large part of the population has become gluten-conscious. Though neither of us are gluten intolerant, we have lots of friends who are—and they have cried on our shoulders about how much they miss pizza, and begged us to create gluten-free pizzas for them.

A funny—and fortuitous—thing happened when we investigated how to bring the pleasures of pizza back to our dearly deprived friends. We discovered that virtually all of the sauces, toppings, and cheeses (as well as our Nibbles & Noshes) in the first edition of this book are naturally gluten-free. This meant that if we could create a gluten-free crust that would stand up to—and be enhanced by—grilling, we could help *glutenistas* enjoy pizza again—a noble culinary challenge if ever there was one.

After 6 months of testing, we zeroed in on two store-bought gluten-free flours, and built a recipe and a technique around them that is the closest thing we have found to the real deal. Is it exactly the same as conventional pizza dough? No. But unlike most of the available store-bought crusts and popular recipes on the Web that hijack the flavors of the toppings, ours is lighter and airier. Sure, the two-step par-bake process requires some effort, but given the alternatives of abstaining from pizza altogether or enduring tooth-cracking crusts, we think the results are SO worth it. The crust we developed is intentionally designed to take on a supporting role—allowing the flavors of the toppings to shine. By choosing gluten-free versions of ingredients, *every pizza recipe* in this edition can be made gluten-free when paired with a gluten-free crust. All the Nibble & Nosh recipes can be made entirely gluten-free with simple substitutions as well.

We didn't stop there. We also jumped on the opportunity to make some additional changes: After demonstrating our direct/indirect grilling technique hundreds of times, we've become better at articulating the critical steps. Here we've fine-tuned the instructions and provided simple-to-follow step-by-step photos. We've also included 10 new pizzas that we're really excited about. They embody our spin on new ingredients and flavor combinations that have recently inspired us.

Now, as we continue our crusade to help pizza-lovers expand their horizons, we can do so with the added conviction that the gods of pizza, just like the higher power, love all of us equally—regardless of our intolerances.

Again, we say Hallelujah!!

Elizabeth   *Bob*

—Elizabeth Karmel and Bob Blumer, 2013

HOW TO USE
THIS BOOK

There is a learning curve to mastering pizza on the grill, but there is no need to be overwhelmed. We've organized this book to make it user friendly. Grilled pizza neophytes should read the Basic Training chapter (page 8) before firing up their grills.

If you have a grill and the will, you can master grilled pizza. The essence of grilled pizza is unquestionably its crispy, slightly smoky crust. Part of the crunchy texture comes from the fact that both sides of the crust are grilled, unlike traditional pizzas, where the top side of the crust is prevented from crisping by the toppings, which are spread directly over the uncooked dough. And because the rustic flavor of a grilled pizza crust is bigger, bolder, and more textural than that of a traditional baked pizza, it lends itself as a base for a wide variety of nontraditional ingredients and flavors. If you take away only one thing from this book, it should be the technique of how to grill the crust. After that, you can wing the rest and we will be content knowing that your pizza-eating life has been enriched.

THE TECHNIQUE

In this section, we teach you the difference between direct and indirect grilling and how that pertains to grilled pizza. Then we give you a step-by-step tutorial for our 1-2-3 Technique, which employs a combination of direct and indirect heat (referred to as the combo method). Everything that you need to know to make great grilled pizza is contained in this technique.

The pizza grilling instructions are clear, concise, and foolproof. If you cook from general grilling cookbooks, you'll notice that our instructions are a little different. We created a new recipe style for *Pizza on the Grill* because switching from direct to indirect heat is the key to the process. You will find easy-to-follow instructions for both gas and charcoal grills, so no griller is left behind. The master instructions can be found on pages 11–17. Refer to these anytime you are unclear about the basic grilling steps.

Speaking of switching, we know that some cooks don't like to flip between sections of a cookbook as they are cooking. If you are one of these, we apologize in advance. We made the decision to simplify and streamline the recipes by relocating all the subrecipes—doughs, sauces, toppings—to The Pantry (page 152). Once you've made a few pizzas and have mastered the 1-2-3 Technique, it is easier to follow the recipe if you can see the list of components all on the same page. This format also reminds you that you need to have all your ingredients made in advance and ready to go before you step up to the grill. Chefs refer to this as *mis en place* (to put in place) and there is no time where this is more important than when making grilled pizza.

The History of Grilled Pizza

The origins of the modern pizza can be traced to a baker named Rafaele Esposito from Naples, Italy. In the late 1800s, Esposito created a pizza to honor Queen Margherita of Savoy and The Margherita was born. The tricolor toppings of basil leaves, fresh mozzarella, and crushed tomato are said to represent the green, white, and red of the Italian flag.

Italian immigrants brought pizza to America: it gained popularity when returning World War II GIs craved the pizza they had eaten and loved in Italy. Pizza moved into the mainstream, and the regional varieties that we know and love flourished. New York became world famous for thin slices, similar to a traditional Neapolitan pizza, and Chicagoans created a deep-dish pie topped with mounds of mozzarella.

In the 1960s, home-delivery service and frozen varieties brought pizza out of restaurants and into the average home. "Gourmet pizzas" evolved from the California restaurant scene in the 1980s, most famously at Wolfgang Puck's Los Angeles restaurant Spago, where wood-fired pizzas were topped with smoked salmon, Brie cheese, wild mushrooms, duck, and other previously unfathomable pizza ingredients. Meanwhile, in Providence, Rhode Island, the proprietors of Al Forno began serving and popularizing grilled pizza following a trip to Italy.

Today, we eat more than three billion pizzas every year—an average of 43 slices for each man, woman, and child in the United States. When you think about crossing the most popular food with the most popular cooking technique, it only makes sense that grilled pizza would captivate our palate. In another example of everything that is old is new again, the crisp, slightly smoky flavor of grilled pizza echoes the traditional Italian versions that the WWII vets brought back to the states with them—bringing twenty-first century pizza back to its nineteenth-century roots, via the outdoor grill.

THE FAB 5 PIZZA COMPONENTS

There are five building blocks that make up grilled pizza: the dough, sauce, toppings, cheese, and finishing touches. Because pizza is so simple and has so few components, it is vital that you use the best-quality raw ingredients. If the quality of any one of them is substandard, the pizza will be a little flat. In Basic Training, we address each of these five components, complete with tips and insider secrets.

OUR SECRET

Even though many of our pizzas have as few as three toppings, we do everything we can to infuse each of them with explosive flavors. We are confident that you will taste the difference.

THE PIZZAS

This book contains 61 of our favorite recipes for grilled pizza; there is something for everyone. Each recipe is accompanied by a recommended beverage pairing—Drink This—though you can take or leave our choice, and the Adventure Club, a suggestion for extra or luxury ingredients or culinary twists to take the recipe one step beyond the ordinary. Because we love grilled pizza so much, we often make a party of it, choosing a menu of three to four pizzas for the night. That's why we have dessert pizzas in addition to our old friends, the classics, as well as our new-fangled creations. And pizza isn't just for lunch or dinner anymore. We've included a few recipes for breakfast and brunch pizzas as well—Sunday mornings will never be the same!

As you page through our pizza recipes, remember taste—and especially combinations of flavors—is totally subjective. So we not only encourage you but in fact we insist that you mix and match, switch toppings around, and substitute your favorite cheeses. If you stumble upon a real winner, we'd love to hear about it. You can email us at pizzaonthegrill@gmail.com.

NIBBLES & NOSHES

One cannot live on pizza alone; one needs a nibble or a nosh to whet the appetite. That's why we've included a number of our favorite little bites to get you started. We created these to accompany, not overwhelm, the main event. They follow our pre-pizza party rule: no cheese, no bread. This collection of olives, nuts, dips, and crudités is savory, satisfying, and fun to eat.

SUPER SALADS

The combination of a grilled pizza and a great salad is absolute dining perfection. The salad provides the fresh, snappy part of the meal; our salads are designed to be eaten before, alongside, and even post-pizza. There is an assortment of styles and flavors to go with all the pizzas.

What Our Icons Mean

Delicious but a bit messy—best eaten with a knife and fork

A pizza any kid will love

One of our top picks for the book—a rock star pizza

PIZZA PANTRY

Our pantry is full of recipes for sauces, precooked topping ingredients, and other referenced items. This section allows for streamlined recipe instructions; any recipe within a recipe has been moved to The Pantry. The dirty little secret for those short on time is that most of these ingredients can be store-bought when time doesn't permit you to make them from scratch. As a special bonus, we've stocked our pantry with some fun extras like our B&E Drizzle-icious Infused Oil, B&E Sprinkle-icious Spice Blend, Beer Can Chicken, and North Carolina–Style Pulled Pork.

WE'RE HERE TO HELP

In addition to these sections, you'll find solutions to common mistakes; our professional secrets to personal pizza success; tips for hosting your own pizza party; menu suggestions; must-have equipment (and there ain't much); and à la carte lists of our favorite toppings, cheeses, and finishing touches to help inspire you when you are ready to strike out on your own beyond the recipes in this book.

Basic Training

If you have a grill and the will, you can master grilled pizza. Our pizzas are defined by their crispy, slightly smoky crust. If you take away only one thing from this book, it should be our technique for grilling the crust. After that you can wing the rest, and we will be content knowing that your pizza-eating life has been enhanced.

CHOOSING A GRILL

The first step to cooking outdoors is choosing your grill. Generally it is a choice based on whether you like the hands-on aspect of building and keeping a fire going in a charcoal grill or flipping a switch (to turn it on) in a gas grill.

GAS VERSUS CHARCOAL

Both charcoal and gas grills are well suited to making grilled pizza and both have their advantages. Our friend David Sanfield opened the Pitfire Pizza Company in Los Angeles a few years ago. In the beginning, he grilled pies over hardwood charcoal, but later he converted to gas—and his pizzas are every bit as awesome.

Given the option, we find that gas grills provide a more consistent heat and better control of the temperature. And their convenience makes it even easier to enjoy grilled pizza whenever the mood strikes: Gas grills must be preheated for 10 to 15 minutes, while it takes up to 30 minutes for charcoal briquettes to be ready for cooking.

The ultimate decision is very personal. Choose the grill that fits your taste and lifestyle—or make the most of the grill you already have.

Understanding Direct and Indirect Grilling

Our 1-2-3 Technique combines the advantages of direct and indirect grilling and delivers the ultimate foolproof grilled pizza—each time, every time. To better master the technique, it is helpful to understand the differences between the two grilling methods.

Direct grilling refers to cooking food directly over the heat source. On a gas grill, this means that all burners are on. On a charcoal grill, it means that the gray-ashed charcoal is spread evenly across the bottom of the grill. The rule of thumb is that any food that cooks in 20 minutes or less—for example a hamburger—should be grilled by the direct method.

Indirect grilling means that there is no heat source directly under the food. This cooking method can only be used with a grill that has a lid, because it's the lid that converts the grill into a convection oven—allowing the heat to circulate around the food. As a rule of thumb, any food that takes more than 20 minutes to cook—for example a whole chicken—should be grilled by the indirect method.

Configuring Grills for Indirect Heat

Gas grill Preheat the grill with all burners on. Then, depending on the number of burners on your grill, you will turn off one or two of them and place the food over the burner(s) you've turned off.

Charcoal grill As a rule, light about 50 briquettes and let burn until covered with a light gray ash. Divide the gray-ashed charcoal evenly (about 25 briquettes per side) on each side of a drip pan and place the food over the drip pan. But *grilled pizza* is an exception.

For grilled pizza, you need to push all the charcoal to one side of the grill and place the food over the side with no charcoal on it. Because the heat is pushed to one side, you will have to rotate the pizza. The reason we recommend the change in technique for grilled pizza is due to the size of the pizza—it is generally too large to fit in between two piles of briquettes and we don't want the edges to burn. If you make smaller pizzas, grill the pizza in the center of the cooking grate with equal amounts of heat on each side.

The Gas Grill Method: Master Instructions

1. Preheat the grill by opening the lid and setting all the burners on high. Close the lid and leave the grill on high for 10 minutes, then reduce the heat of all the burners to medium.

2. While the grill preheats, sprinkle your work surface generously with grits or polenta. We find that a cutting board, the back of a sheet pan, or a pizza peel works best. Place the dough in the middle of the surface and roll in the grits until the ball is evenly dusted. Drizzle the dough generously with oil (the oil helps generate the crispy crust). Then roll out the dough with a rolling pin, stretch it out with your hands, or press it out from the center against the work surface. Your ultimate goal is to get the dough ⅛ to ¼ inch thick. Shape your dough according to your grill configuration (see the diagram on page 12). Don't worry about making it perfect—organically shaped crusts are part of the charm of grilled pizza.

The 1-2-3 Technique for Gas-Grilled Pizza

Before you start, preheat the grill by opening the lid and setting all the burners on high. Close the lid and leave on high for 10 minutes.

1 Set all burners to medium and place the dough on the cooking grate. Close the lid and cook until the bottom is golden brown, 3 to 5 minutes.

2 Remove the crust from the grill using tongs and a pizza peel or rimless baking sheet, and flip it to reveal the grilled side. Spread the entire grilled surface with the sauce, add toppings, and sprinkle with cheese.

3 Reconfigure the grill to indirect heat. (If you have a two-burner grill, turn off one burner. For three- or four-burner grills, turn off the center burner or burners.) Transfer the pizza back onto the grate over the unlit section, close the lid, and grill until the bottom is golden brown and crispy, and the cheese is bubbly, 7 to 10 minutes.

3. Transfer your dough to the grilling area—we find that a pizza peel does this job the best—and pick it up by the two corners closest to you. In one motion, lay it down flat on the cooking grate from back to front (as you would set a tablecloth down on a table).

4. Close the lid and grill for 3 minutes (no peeking!), then check the crust and, if necessary, continue grilling until the bottom is well marked and golden brown. If your grill cooks unevenly, finesse the bottom by rotating the crust and/or moving it to another section of the grill. Once you become comfortable making pizza on the grill, this part of the process will become second nature to you and will contribute to a perfectly cooked pizza.

5. Once the bottom is well browned, use tongs to transfer the crust from the grill to the pizza peel or rimless baking sheet, then immediately close the lid of the grill; this will keep the grill at the ideal temperature. Flip the crust to reveal the grilled side. Follow the specific recipe directions for adding sauce, toppings, and/or cheese.

6. Before returning your pizza to the grill, switch the grill to indirect heat. (For a two-burner grill, turn off one burner. For three- or four-burner grills, turn off the center burner or burners.) Transfer the pizza onto the grate over the unlit section and close the lid. Grill until the bottom is golden brown and crispy, and the cheese is melted, 7 to 10 minutes. For two-burner grills, rotate the pizza 180 degrees after 5 minutes.

7. Remove the finished pizza from the grill, garnish, and season as directed. Slice and serve immediately.

Shaping Your Dough to Fit Your Gas Grill

The type of grill you have is going to affect how you shape your pizzas. Why? Because to avoid scorching the crust, the dough should not stray over the direct heat source—it should sit entirely over the indirect heat section of your grill. For gas grills, you'll need to know the burner configuration of your particular grill.

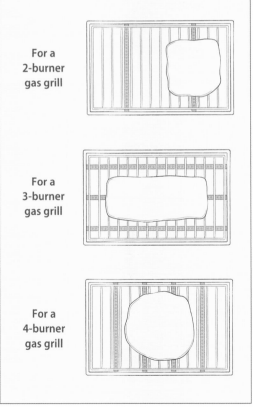

For a
2-burner
gas grill

For a
3-burner
gas grill

For a
4-burner
gas grill

THE GAS GRILL METHOD: Step-by-Step

Roll dough in grits.

Drizzle with oil.

Stretch by hand...

...or roll.

Transfer to peel.

Bring peel to grill.

Place over direct heat.

Let bubbles form.

Check bottom for doneness.

Remove crust from grill.

Flip and top.

Return to indirect heat.

The Charcoal Grill Method: Master Instructions

1. Build a fire by lighting 50 to 60 charcoal briquettes in either a chimney starter or in a pyramid-shaped mound on the bottom grate of your grill. Once the briquettes have become gray-ashed (20 to 30 minutes), move them all to one side of the grill.

2. While the grill preheats, sprinkle your work surface—we find that a cutting board, a sheet pan, or a pizza peel works best—generously with grits or polenta. Place the dough in the middle of the surface and roll in the grits until the ball is evenly dusted. Drizzle the dough generously with oil (it's the oil that helps generate the crispy crust). Then roll out the dough with a rolling pin, stretch it out with your hands, or press it out from the center against the work surface. Your ultimate goal is to get the dough ⅛ to ¼ inch thick. Stretch your dough into a rectangular or oblong shape (see the diagram on page 15). Don't worry about making it perfect—organically shaped crusts are part of the charm of grilled pizza.

3. Transfer your dough to the grilling area—a pizza peel does this job the best—and pick it up by the two corners closest to you. In one motion, lay it down flat—over the side of the grill without briquettes—on the cooking grate from back to front (as you would set a tablecloth down on a table). Close the lid and grill for 4 minutes (no peeking!), then rotate the crust 180 degrees and continue grilling until the bottom is well marked and golden brown, another 2 to 3 minutes. You may need to finesse the bottom by rotating the crust again, and/or shifting its position slightly. Once you become comfortable making pizza on the grill, this part of the process will become second nature to you and will contribute to a perfectly cooked, crispy pizza.

The 1-2-3 Technique for Charcoal Grilled Pizza

Before you start, build a charcoal fire and arrange the gray-ashed briquettes for indirect grilling by moving them to one side, making sure not to cover the air vent.

1 Place the dough on the cooking grate over the side without briquettes, close the lid, and grill for 4 minutes, then rotate the crust 180 degrees and continue grilling until the bottom is well marked and evenly browned.

2 Remove the crust from the grill using tongs and a pizza peel or rimless cookie sheet and flip it to reveal the grilled side. Spread the entire grilled surface with the sauce, add toppings, and sprinkle with cheese.

3 Transfer the pizza back onto the grate over the unlit section, close the lid, and grill until the bottom is golden brown and crispy, and the cheese is bubbly, 7 to 10 minutes. Rotate 180 degrees after 5 minutes.

4. Once the bottom is well browned, use tongs to transfer the crust from the grill to your pizza peel or rimless baking sheet, then immediately close the lid of the grill; this will keep the grill at the ideal temperature. Flip the crust to reveal the grilled side. Follow the specific recipe directions for adding sauce, toppings, and/or cheese.

5. Transfer the pizza back onto the grate over the side without briquettes and grill, with the lid on, for 4 to 5 minutes. Rotate the pizza 180 degrees and continue to grill with the lid on until the bottom is golden brown and crispy, and the cheese is melted, another 4 to 5 minutes.

6. Remove the finished pizza from the grill, garnish, and season as directed. Slice and serve immediately.

Shaping Your Dough to Fit Your Charcoal Grill

For a charcoal grill, shape your dough into a rectangular or oblong shape, but don't make it as large as you would if you have a gas grill. Only a portion of the dough will reach to the center of the grill, which is the widest part, since you'll want the dough sitting entirely over the indirect heat section of your grill.

For No-Fail Charcoal Grilling

A cast-iron pizza pan is a charcoal griller's insurance policy against burning the crust. If you are using one of these pans, spread the gray-ashed charcoal in a single layer over the charcoal grate and set the pizza pan in the center of the cooking grate. Close the lid and preheat as directed for 5 minutes, then follow the steps for charcoal, cooking the pizza on the pizza pan instead of directly on the cooking grate.

The Grill/Oven Combo Method: Master Instructions

This method is perfect for parties and other occasions when you want to do most of the work ahead of time and finish the pizza in your kitchen.

1. Follow the Gas or Charcoal Method directions for cooking the first side of the crust.

2. Use tongs to turn the crust over. Grill until the other side is set, but not browned, 1 to 2 minutes.

3. Transfer the crust from the grill to a pizza peel or rimless baking sheet and reserve until ready for use (grilled dough will hold at room temperature for several hours or a day if refrigerated). If you are pregrilling dough more than an hour in advance, wait until it has cooled to room temperature then wrap it in plastic wrap.

4. About 30 minutes before serving your pizza, position a rack in the center of the oven and preheat to 450°F. Put the crust in the oven, browned side up, for 3 to 4 minutes to recrisp.

5. Transfer the crisped crust from the oven to a pizza peel or rimless baking sheet, keeping the browned side up. Follow the specific recipe directions for adding sauce, toppings, and/or cheese.

6. Transfer the pizza back onto the center oven rack and bake until the bottom is golden brown and crispy, and the cheese is melted, 7 to 10 minutes.

7. Remove from the oven, garnish, and season as directed. Slice and serve immediately.

The Oven-Only Method: Master Instructions:

This method is for city slickers without a grill, for cooking in subzero temperatures, or for occasions when you run out of gas.

1. Position a rack in the center of oven. Preheat the oven to 450°F.

2. While the oven preheats, sprinkle your work surface—we find that a cutting board, a sheet pan, or a pizza peel works best—generously with grits or polenta. Place the dough in the middle of the surface and roll in the grits until the ball is evenly dusted. Drizzle the dough generously with oil (it's the oil that helps generate the crispy crust). Then roll out the dough with a rolling pin, stretch it out with your hands, or press it out from the center against the work surface. Your ultimate goal is to get the dough ⅛ to ¼ inch thick. Don't worry about making it perfect—organically shaped crusts are part of the charm of grilled pizza.

3. Slide out the oven rack. Pick up the dough by the two corners closest to you. In one motion, lay it down flat directly on the rack from back to front. Slide the rack back into the oven, close the door, and bake for 10 minutes (you can peek through the window but don't open the door). Check the crust and, if necessary, continue baking until the bottom is well marked and golden brown. If your oven cooks unevenly, you may need to finesse the bottom by rotating the crust and/or moving it to another area of the rack. Once you become comfortable making pizza in your oven, this part of the process will become second nature to you and will contribute to a perfectly cooked, crispy pizza.

4. Use tongs to transfer the crust to a pizza peel or rimless baking sheet and close the oven door. Flip the crust to reveal the browned side. Follow the specific recipe directions for adding sauce, topping, and/or cheese.

5. Transfer the pizza back onto the center oven rack and bake until the bottom is golden brown and crispy, and the cheese is melted, 7 to 10 minutes.

6. Remove from the oven, garnish, and season as directed. Slice and serve immediately.

KNOW YOUR DOUGH

The dough is the most important part of grilled pizza, even though it is the component we fuss over the least. Oiling the dough, dusting it with grits or polenta, and grilling gives an intense flavor to just about any type of dough you choose to start with.

In our formative years, we bought our dough from Domino's® or any other pizza joint where the employee would happily pocket a couple of bucks in return for a ball or two. Nobody knew it wasn't made from scratch—it was our little shortcut. These days, your options for store-bought dough are much greater. Trader Joe's℠ sells it fresh for a buck a ball (and has several varieties to boot), other grocery stores carry it fresh and frozen, and more and more bakeries and pizzerias sell it as well.

Making dough from scratch is like making homemade stock. If you've got the time and the

Dough Add-ins

Every once in a while, when we want to pull out all the stops, we add flavor enhancers to our dough before we grill it. These crusts take pizza one step further; on their own, they make lovely appetizers, especially when topped with cheese. Knead one or more of the following ingredients into your homemade or store-bought dough to make a fancy and flavorful pizza crust or flatbread.

Herbs—chopped or whole fresh leaves, or dried

Garlic—chopped or sliced fresh, or dehydrated

Olives—chopped, sliced, or whole

Bacon or lardon—cooked till crisp

Hard cheese—freshly grated Parmigiano-Reggiano, Pecorino, or your favorite hard cheese

Nuts—chopped walnuts or hazelnuts, sunflower seeds, pine nuts, etc.

Citrus zest—grated lemon, lime, or orange

Scallions—both white and green parts, sliced

Dried fruit—raisins, currants, cherries, etc.

Sweet chips—chocolate, cinnamon, or peanut butter

inclination, why not make it? In The Pantry, on pages 152 to 181, we provide you with more than 40 easy-to-make recipes (including our gluten-free dough) to help you stake your claim as a baker. And while you are at it, make extra and freeze it in individual-sized balls (about 8 ounces each). If properly wrapped, frozen dough, whether home-made or store-bought, will last for up to 6 months and is every bit as good as fresh. When using frozen dough, allow about 2 hours for it to thaw (unrefrigerated) and an additional hour for it to come up to room temperature.

Size it up Your ball of dough should be the size of a softball, about 4 inches in diameter and 8 ounces in weight. This will yield one medium (12- to 14-inch) individual pizza—enough for two people as a meal or four as an appetizer.

Relax it Dough should be taken out of the refrigerator 1 hour before use and allowed to "relax." Frozen dough needs 2 hours to thaw (unrefrigerated), in addition to another hour to come to room temperature.

Roll with it To roll out your dough, sprinkle a clean work surface generously with polenta or grits. This will prevent it from sticking to the surface. We prefer polenta or grits (they're the same thing—stone-ground corn—just different terminology) to flour because it gives the pizza a more rustic texture. Grits and polenta are available in both yellow and white varieties. Roll dough in the grits until the ball is evenly dusted. Drizzle the dough generously with olive oil (it's the oil that helps generate the crispy crust). Then roll out the dough with a rolling pin, stretch it out with your hands, or press it out from the cen-

ter against the work surface. Shape your dough according to your grill configuration (see the diagrams on pages 12 and 15). Don't worry about making it perfect—organically shaped crusts are part of the charm of grilled pizza, and we think they taste better.

Thin is in Dough rises as it grills. To ensure a final result that is thin and crispy, roll, stretch or press out the dough to ⅛ to ¼ inch in thickness.

Keep it supple When not working with the dough, keep it lightly coated with olive oil and covered with a clean tea towel or plastic wrap to prevent the exterior from drying out or cracking.

Burst its bubble When you place the raw dough on the grill to cook the first side of the crust, giant bubbles may form. This is a sign that the yeast is active and the dough is rising—that's a good thing. You can allow small bubbles to remain, adding even more organic charm to the crust. Pop the large ones with tongs like we do.

Put a lid on it The residual heat that has built up inside your grill while it preheated (with the lid down) and the direct heat from the burners will make the crust rise. The quicker you can put the crust on the grill and close the lid, the lighter and crispier the pizza will be.

THE SAUCE

Sauce makes a pizza a pizza. Without it, it would be cheese toast or an open-faced sandwich. Sauce also anchors the pizza, holding the toppings and cheese together and adding great mouth-feel. It provides a flavor dimension that sometimes balances the richness of the cheese and sometimes provides the richness itself.

If you can spread it, it can be used as a pizza sauce. There is almost no limit to what can be spread. In The Pantry (see page 152), you'll find a full range of sauces, from vine-ripened tomato to roasted garlic paste to pesto in multiple aromatic forms. When time is limited, use best-quality store-bought pizza sauce or crushed tomatoes right out of the can in place of homemade sauce or purchase ready-made versions of many of the other spreads.

THE
TOPPINGS

It wasn't that many years ago when the list of toppings found on pizza was relatively short and very conventional. Then Wolfgang Puck put smoked salmon on his pizza at Spago and all hell broke loose. Now we are only limited by our imaginations. If there is a food you love, chances are you can build a pizza around it. The more flavorful the toppings, the tastier the pizza will be. So be sure to season each ingredient to maximize its flavor potential (but be careful not to oversalt, since every component is salted and cheese is inherently salty).

The short time it takes to grill the pizza will only warm the toppings and melt the cheese. Therefore, as with any conventionally baked pizza, all pizza toppings must either be edible raw or be precooked.

Refer to our list of popular toppings for inspiration, and try a selection from The Pantry, such as Fire-Roasted Cherry Tomatoes (page 167) or shredded Beer Can Chicken (page 168).

THE
CHEESES

Just as clothes make the man, cheese definitely defines the pizza. In the early days of pizza making, mozzarella was used because of its price and availability. To this day, mozzarella is still the cheese of choice in most pizzerias. But with the increasing selection of cheeses available in most grocery stores—or if you are lucky enough to live close to a local cheese shop—there is now a world of cheeses at your fingertips. Specialty cheeses can elevate your pizza to a whole new level. Think of today's pizza as a new kind of cheese course. Some of our favorites are imported Italian Parmigiano-Reggiano, Fontina, French triple crèmes, the Swiss family, and the big blues (Stilton, Roquefort, Gorgonzola, and Cabrales).

Not all cheeses act in the same way when exposed to high heat. Fresh cheeses with high water content, like mozzarella and ricotta, don't melt with the same ooey-gooey texture as aged cheeses; nor do low-fat cheeses. And not all cheeses melt evenly, which can be a good thing, adding to the texture and appeal of the pizza. Some cheese should be sliced, while others perform better when grated or crumbled. Sometimes the rind adds flavor; other times it can act as a hindrance, as when the rind prevents the cheese from spreading beyond its edge.

Great Pizza Cheeses

- Asiago
- Blue cheese, crumbled
- Brie, sliced ¼ inch thick, with the rind on or off
- Camembert, sliced ¼ inch thick, with the rind on or off
- Cheddar, grated
- Comté, grated
- Fontina, grated
- Goat cheese (chèvre), fresh and aged, sliced or spooned
- Gorgonzola, crumbled
- Gouda, grated
- Gruyère, grated
- Locatelli®, grated
- Mascarpone
- Mozzarella, dried, grated
- Mozzarella, fresh, sliced
- Parmigiano-Reggiano (Parmesan), grated finely
- Pecorino romano, grated finely
- Provolone, grated
- Ricotta
- Robiola
- Smoked Cheddar, grated
- St. André
- Stilton, crumbled

When purchasing cheese for pizza, don't cut corners. Look for the best quality and don't be afraid to spend a few bucks—you don't need that much per pizza. There are lots of artisanal cheese producers in the United States making cheese in the European tradition. A few of our favorites are Cowgirl Creamery®, Cypress Grove®, Point Reyes, Maytag Blue, and Coach Farms™. Unfortunately, some American versions of European cheeses like Parmigiano-Reggiano still cannot compete with the original.

FINISHING TOUCHES

One of the big differences between a good cook and a great cook is how he or she finishes a dish. The final seasoning or flavor enhancer, when correctly selected, can add another dimension to the dish and give it that "finishing touch." The last thing you put on the pizza is the first thing the diner tastes, so whatever you are adding needs to taste fresh and clean. The classic finishing touches are best-quality salt and olive oil. But we don't always stop there. Infused oils, spices, and fresh herbs all lend themselves perfectly to grilled pizza. We've combined our favorite flavors into our own signature B&E Drizzle-icious Infused Oil and B&E Sprinkle-icious Spice Blend, which can be used on virtually any pizza (see page 180). Other flavored oils worth trying include garlic, truffle, toasted sesame, roasted hazelnut, roasted walnut, lemon, and hot chile.

Try other tasty sprinkles such as fleur de sel or your favorite specialty salt (Maldon, sel gris, pink, black, etc.), freshly ground pepper, chopped fresh herbs (chives, basil, tarragon, mint, parsley, cilantro, etc.), red pepper flakes, sesame seeds, toasted nuts, finely grated citrus zest, capers, minced fresh garlic or roasted garlic cloves, or dried herbs (oregano, rosemary, thyme, and herbes de Provence).

THE EQUIPMENT

The beauty of grilled pizza is that there are so few barriers to entry. All it really takes is a grill and the will. That said, there are a few tools that can make your life (at least as it pertains to grilling pizza) easier. We've prioritized them for you so that as your interest in grilled pizza turns into an addiction, you can add to your arsenal of tools.

MUST HAVE
- Grill and fuel

NICE TO HAVE
- Pizza peel or rimless baking sheet
- Tongs
- Sharp knife, kitchen scissors, or pizza wheel
- Pastry brush for applying oil
- Rolling pin
- Silicone spatula for spreading sauces
- Grilling mitt
- Cheese grater (we love Microplanes!)

LUXURIOUS TO HAVE
- Cast-iron or ceramic pizza pan (our favorites are made by Lodge and Emile Henri)
- Food processor or stand mixer for making dough
- Food processor or blender for making sauces, pastes, and spreads
- Food mill for making tomato sauces
- Multiple peels for serving and for pizza parties—check out Elizabeth's products at elizabethkarmel.com
- A nice bottle of wine to sip on while you stand by your grill

PROFESSIONAL SECRETS

If we were hovering behind you in your backyard as you were grilling pizza for the first time, these are the crucial steps and pointers that we would shout out.

Throw away your pizza stone Our grilled pizza technique requires nothing more than the grates on your grill.

Practice To avoid the stress of learning a new dish in front of a crowd, practice alone. When your guests arrive, you'll surprise them with your confidence and expertise.

Be prepared Before your guests arrive, have your dough rolled out and your toppings precooked, cut, and grated.

Beg, borrow, or steal Use the best-quality ingredients you can get your mitts on. Beyond mastering the technique of grilling the crust, this is the single most important thing you can do to elevate the quality of your pizza. Why? Because grilled pizza is a very simple, uncomplicated food. It is little more than a thin layer of crusty bread with sauce, toppings, and cheese. With every bite, you can literally taste each ingredient. The best pizzas explode (in your mouth) with flavor.

Combine two or more cheeses per pizza Even a simple cheese pizza can be elevated to gourmet status when you combine two or more quality cheeses that have different flavor profiles. For example, imported Italian Parmigiano-Reggiano adds sharpness, fresh mozzarella adds creaminess, and goat cheese adds earthiness when paired with other cheeses.

Stretch or roll out your dough as thin as possible For the thinnest pizza, let your dough rise to room temperature before rolling or stretching it out. After you have rolled it out, let it relax for several minutes, then stretch it a final time.

Use uncooked polenta or coarse-ground uncooked grits to create a rustic texture This is our preference and what we call for in most of our recipes. If you find the texture too gritty for your taste, replace it with fine-grain cornmeal or flour.

Shape the pizza to fit within the boundaries of your indirect heat source This is an important step since our 1-2-3 Technique calls for switching the heat source from direct to indirect before grilling the fully loaded pizza. The shape of your dough is crucial because any part of the pizza that overlaps a direct heat source will char before the pizza finishes cooking.

Brush rolled-out crust generously with olive oil on both sides The oil will facilitate crispness and eliminate stickage.

Create organic shapes We think irregularly shaped pizza tastes better—at least to the eyes. We also embrace the natural holes that develop in the dough both when we stretch it and while it is rising and bubbling on the grill.

Preheat the grill Your dough will not rise unless you place it in a hot environment on hot preheated cooking grates. Be patient; it will take about 10 minutes for a gas grill to preheat. For charcoal, allow 20 to 30 minutes for the flames to die out and the charcoal to be covered with a white-gray ash.

Read between the lines If your grill is too hot, the grill marks on your raw dough will quickly blacken and char, not turn golden brown as desired. If your grill has hot and cold spots, you will need to rotate your crust halfway through the cooking time for it to brown evenly.

Keep a lid on it Leave the lid down for 3 to 4 minutes (no peeking!) before checking on the crust to maximize the initial rise of the dough. Keep the lid closed at all times to conserve the heat—especially between steps 1 and 2 when you remove pizza to add toppings.

Spread the ingredients evenly and generously Make every slice of the pizza a "best bite." (After all, you never know which slice you are going to end up with!)

Test for doneness There are two visual clues for doneness. The first is the cheese. It should be fully melted and may be bubbling. If your pizza has mostly fresh cheese like ricotta on it, use the crust to test for doneness. For the crust test, you can either look underneath it to see if the bottom is golden brown or test its flexibility. To do this, lift and slightly bend the crust with your tongs. If the dough bends, keep cooking. If it is rigid and crisp, it is ready to come off the grill.

Finish it with flair When correctly selected, the final seasoning, or "finishing touch" as we call it, can add another dimension to the dish. The classic finishing touches are best-quality salt and olive oil, but don't stop there. Infused oils, spices, fresh herbs, and citrus zest are perfect finishing touches for grilled pizza. Try our signature B&E Drizzle-icious Infused Oil and B&E Sprinkle-icious Spice Blend on page 180.

Chop chop We prefer our pizza cut in squares. However you choose to slice it, have your cutting tools at the ready. Grilled pizza is best served hot and crispy, right off the grill.

Common Problems & Solutions

PROBLEM	SOLUTION
Crust is too thick	Sorry, Charlie, if your crust is already cooked, it's too late this time. Next time, stretch or roll out the dough thinner than you think it needs to be.
Pizza is burnt	You can't fix this now. Next time, cook your pizza entirely over medium indirect heat (page 10) to ensure that the pizza crust won't burn. If you are using indirect heat to finish cooking your pizza but the outer edges of your crust burn, your dough may not be properly shaped to fit your burner configuration. (Refer to Shaping Your Dough to Fit Your Grill on pages 12 and 15.)
Fire is too hot and bottom of crust instantly burns	Immediately remove the dough from the grates and leave the lid open for a few minutes to cool off the grates and the interior of the grill. For charcoal grills, never place the dough over flaming charcoal. Wait until the charcoal is covered with a white-gray ash. For gas grills, reduce the heat to medium.
Crust is undercooked	Continue cooking over indirect heat. For future pizzas, roll out the dough as thin as possible and grill the topped pizza over indirect heat for as long as necessary. The bottom of the crust should be firm and crisp when it is cooked through. Generally, the crust will be cooked through by the time the cheese is melted and bubbly.
Cheese won't melt and/or toppings are cold	Be patient and continue cooking over indirect heat. And always make sure you close the lid of your grill completely.
Toppings don't cook during grilling	Precook or pregrill all raw toppings before making your pizza; the pizza is on the grill such a short time there is not enough time or heat to cook toppings from a raw state.
Crust cooks before toppings are prepped	Grilled pizzas cook faster than a fire in a match factory. As with any recipe that cooks quickly, you must be well organized and have everything prepared in advance (mis en place).

Going Gluten-Free

If you have celiac disease or are gluten-intolerant (or cooking for someone who is), this section is for you. It contains all the information you need to ensure that anything you make from this book can be gluten-free.

Beyond the dough substitution, we've recommended ingredients that are gluten-free—and the number of available gluten-free products is growing. You should always check product labels, though, to ensure there are no hidden glutens. We hope you will enjoy cooking from this book with the enhanced confidence of knowing that you can enjoy every recipe from it.

The awareness for gluten intolerance has changed dramatically since we wrote the first edition of this book in 2007. To fully appreciate the phenomenon, all you need to do is walk down the aisle of any grocery store and marvel at the myriad gluten-free options.

The gluten-free world is made up of people with celiac disease who must eliminate all traces of glutens, and those with a gluten intolerance who do their best to minimize their intake of glutens. If you are reading this section, chances are you either fall into one of these categories or are cooking for someone who does. It is our goal to make the world of grilled pizza accessible to all those who are affected by gluten, and to make them happy—very happy. That said, as excited as we are to make pizza on the grill for our gluten-free friends, we do not want to misrepresent this book or ourselves. This book is primarily a cookbook devoted to the craft and enjoyment of pizza on the grill. To be clear, the book was not written as a gluten-free or allergy-free pizza cookbook, nor does it address the issues of those with multiple allergies.

Neither of us is gluten-intolerant (though we are intolerant in many other ways!), but we are both well versed in cooking around myriad allergies, intolerances, and plain old dislikes. When we were asked to review our original 50 grilled pizza recipes to determine which ones could be adapted to a gluten-free crust, we were prepared to unearth a veritable Pandora's box. Much to our surprise—and delight—we discovered that virtually all of the ingredients we called for in the original edition of this book are either intrinsically gluten-free or *can* be with a simple substitu-

tion of brands. If you have celiac disease or severe allergies to corn, soy, casein, and/or diary, you will need to be vigilant, and edit and substitute these recipes as you normally do.

When it comes to pizza on the grill, *the difference between gluten-rich and gluten-free is almost entirely in the crust.* Consequently, our main challenge was to develop the best-possible gluten-free crust. We started by testing all of the widely distributed brands of gluten-free flours, ranging from all-purpose flours to those dedicated specifically to pizza. In all cases we followed the directions on the box. The results were less than satisfactory. The majority of the products we tasted had a vegetal aftertaste and lacked the rise we were looking for. We toyed around with making our own flours, but decided it was too cumbersome and labor-intensive—and in conflict with our mission to simplify, not complicate, your life. In the name of pizza equality for all, we pressed forward.

Starting with our two favorite flours (Thomas Kellar's C4C and King Arthur's Gluten-Free Multi-Purpose Flour), we tried making our basic dough recipe (page 154). That worked satisfactorily with Thomas Kellar's C4C but not for the King Arthur flour—and neither measured up to our hopes and aspirations. Since a lack of glutens translates directly into a lack of stretch, our quest was to add body and rise, as well as flavor and texture that best mimicked conventional pizza dough.

After months of testing various combinations and permutations of additional ingredients, we settled on a recipe that incorporated baking powder for leavening, xanthan gum to bind, extra yeast to help the rise, and an egg yolk to add tenderness to the "crumb." The result yielded the best-tasting, most pleasingly textured gluten-free dough we have tasted (page 158).

Once we cracked the ingredient code, our next challenge was to adapt the dough to the grill. Because of the nature of gluten-free dough—which is extremely delicate and sticky before it is cooked—it is difficult to put the uncooked dough directly on the cooking grates as we do with our basic dough. (Note: We discovered some direct-to-grill dough recipes on the Web, but they were all either impractical or, even worse, inedible.) After more trial and error, we created a two-step process: the first step involves rolling out the dough on a sheet pan, letting it rise, and then par-baking it in an oven for 10 minutes. The second step involves transferring the dough to the grill where it is then handled and grilled in a similar manner to our traditional grilled crust. Sure this technique requires an extra step, but we assume that if you are fed up with having to sacrifice one of life's great pleasures, you will be willing go the extra distance in order to create a guilt-free crust you can trust.

With the dough issue solved, we circled back to the toppings and analyzed every sauce, topping, and cheese in the book in order to identify any ingredient that could possibly contain glutens. (Note: The more processed a food is—especially where starch modifiers and emulsifiers are used— the more likely it is to contain glutens.) Where no gluten-free option was available, we modified our original recipe. Where the potential for hidden glutens exists, we recommend you scrutinize it before using, and if necessary search out another

Gluten-Free Flour Power

Most gluten-free flours on the market are made with a combination of gluten-free ingredients derived from chickpeas, white rice, brown rice, tapioca, corn, and potatoes. Some have additional ingredients added such as xanthan gum, milk powder, and dried egg. Though they are all made from the same pool of ingredients, they do not all taste, smell, or perform the same way.

After testing many brands, our favorite was a collaboration between Thomas Keller (of French Laundry fame) and Lena Kwak, called C4C Gluten-Free flour. C4C stands for cup for cup. As the name suggests, it is designed to replace conventional flour at a perfect cup-for-cup ratio. New to the market is the C4C Gluten-Free Pizza Crust Mix. We highly recommend leaping tall buildings or doing whatever it takes to get your mitts on some. King Arthur Flour® Gluten-Free Multi-Purpose Flour is the only other brand that delivered acceptable results.

At the time of this writing, C4C is available at select specialty stores including William Sonoma, Wegman's, Whole Foods, and Dean and Deluca or via the Internet. Each bag will make approximately seven 12-inch pizza crusts. Stock up.

brand (see a list of common ingredients that you need to scrutinize on the facing page). As a result of our revisions, any pizza in this edition, when made with our gluten-free crust and gluten-free toppings, can be made to be gluten-free.

Now, if you are vigilant, you can have your grilled pizza *and* eat it too!

Technique for grilling gluten-free dough after the par-bake step

At every stage in the process, be careful when handling the dough. All gluten-free dough is fragile and may split.

1. If your dough is frozen, thaw before using.

2. Brush both sides generously with olive oil and sprinkle with grits or polenta.

3. Follow our master grilling instructions for gas (page 11) or charcoal (page 14) with one exception—the first side should be grilled slightly longer to brown, about 6 minutes over direct medium heat.

4. Flip the pizza crust over and top the grilled side with sauce, toppings, and cheese. Finish cooking over indirect medium heat until the bottom of the crust is nicely browned, the toppings are hot, and the cheese is melted and bubbling.

Ingredients in this book that may contain gluten

I f you or someone you are cooking for is gluten-intolerant, make sure to scrutinize the labels of all ingredients you purchase. The ingredients identified in the list here have been selected with the best research available to us, and are based on versions of the products we call for at the time of writing this revised edition. Because products are constantly being reformulated, you need to take ownership of your situation and remain vigilant.

- Tomato sauce
- Sausage of all kinds
- Pesto
- White bean purée
- Balsamic
- Dairy:
  - crème fraîche
  - yogurt
  - mascarpone
  - sour cream
  - cream cheese
  - ricotta
  - boursin
  - ice cream
  - whipped cream
- Olive tapenade
- Nutella®
- Tomato salsa
- Smoked salmon
- Chipotles in adobo

- Quince paste
- Truffle oil
- Fig jam
- BBQ sauce
- Vinegar sauce
- Caesar salad dressing
- Marmalade
- Peanut butter
- White chocolate
- Heath® bar
- Dolce de leche sauce
- Caramel sauce
- Sriracha sauce
- Dry-roasted peanuts
- Hoisen (xanthan gum)
- Toasted sesame seeds
- Major Grey's chutney
- Horseradish cream sauce
- Dill pickles
- Refried beans

- Tabasco®
- Pepper vodka
- Capers
- Anchovies
- Crab meat
- Worcestershire sauce
- Dijon
- Mango purée
- Shredded coconut
- Tamari
- Dry mustard
- Red-wine vinegar
- Tahini
- Dehydrated herbs

GLUTEN-FREE DOUGH: Step-by-Step

Make dough, let rise.

Oil pan, sprinkle with grits.

Spread dough and oil.

Sprinkle dough with grits.

Cover and let rise.

Bake in oven.

Brush with oil.

Grill prebaked crust.

Check for doneness.

Flip, then add toppings.

Return to grill.

Slice and enjoy!

Gluten-Free Pizza Dough Alternatives

PORTABELLA MUSHROOMS

Portabellas are nature's own individual-size deep-dish pizzas. They are a natural with any combination of veggie toppings and will add an interesting layer of flavor to meaty pizzas such as our Black 'n' Blue Steak or Greens on White pies.

To prepare: De-stem a large portabella. In a small bowl, combine 2 tablespoons olive oil, 2 teaspoons balsamic vinegar, 1 minced clove garlic, and salt and pepper. Brush the gill side of the mushroom generously with the vinaigrette and let it rest for 10 minutes. Grill, gill side down, for 10 minutes over medium heat. Flip, then reconfigure the grill to indirect heat, top the mushroom with your desired ingredients, and continue grilling with the lid down for 8 minutes, or until the cheese is bubbling.

CORN TORTILLAS

Corn tortillas, especially the thick versions, make perfect individual-size thin-crust pizzas. In fact, their inherent flavors will even enhance certain combinations such as our Nacho Libre, Queso Fundido, and Blistered Corn, Asparagus & Pesto pizzas.

To prepare: Brush lightly with corn oil, then grill one side over direct heat for 2 minutes. Flip, then reconfigure the grill to indirect heat, top the tortilla with your desired ingredients, and continue grilling with the lid down for about 8 minutes, or until the cheese is bubbling and the bottom is crispy.

Note: Not all corn tortillas are gluten-free. Read the ingredients carefully.

ROASTED POTATO SLICES

Potato slices made perfect "crusts" for tapas-style mini pizzas.

To prepare: Slice a large russet potato lengthwise into ¼-inch-thick slices. Brush both sides with olive oil and bake on a sheet pan in a 350°F oven, or on the grill over indirect heat for 20 minutes, or until browned on both sides and cooked through. Turn once. Top browned slices with sauce, toppings, and cheese, and grill over indirect heat with the lid down for 8 minutes, or until the cheese is bubbling.

READY-MADE CRUST OPTIONS

• Gluten-free frozen waffles (for dessert pizzas, Dixie Chicken)
• Gluten-free English muffins
• Gluten-free pita
• Gluten-free flatbreads

The Pizzas

Now the fun really begins! We´ve created more than 60 diverse and delicious pizzas oozing with unctuous cheese and bursting with flavor. Anyway you slice it, there is something here for everyone. Ladies and gentlemen, start your grills!

THE CLASSICS

The classics are so-named classic because they just can't be beat.
We've put our own spin on pizza parlor standards to make them the new classics.

Queen Margherita Pizza

Serves 2 to 4 😊

The original pizza was created by an Italian baker from Naples in honor of Queen Margherita. The red, white, and green ingredients were his homage to the Italian flag. The beauty of a Margherita is in the simplicity of its fresh ingredients. When you get down to it, it is basically uncooked crushed tomatoes, creamy mozzarella cheese, and fragrant fresh basil.

¼   cup uncooked grits or polenta, for rolling the dough

1   ball prepared pizza dough, at room temperature

2   tablespoons olive oil

1   cup Crushed Tomato Sauce (page 160)

1   large clove garlic, minced

8   ounces fresh mozzarella cheese, cut into ¼-inch-thick slices (or 1 cup grated if fresh is unavailable)

10 fresh basil leaves

Kosher salt and freshly ground black pepper to taste

Preheat the grill, roll out and shape the dough, and grill the first side of the crust per the master instructions on page 11 for gas or page 14 for charcoal. Use tongs to transfer it to a peel or rimless baking sheet. Flip the crust to reveal the grilled side.

Spread the entire surface with the sauce, sprinkle with the garlic, and top with the cheese.

Finish grilling the pizza per the master instructions.

Remove from the grill, garnish with the basil, and season with salt and pepper. Slice and serve immediately.

ADVENTURE CLUB Use genuine buffalo mozzarella or burrata, a really creamy mozzarella-like cheese.

DRINK THIS Chianti Classico is a popular wine from Tuscany made from the sangiovese grape. Its high acid content makes it a natural pairing for Italian dishes or any dish that features naturally acidic tomato sauce.

All-American Pepperoni Pizza

Serves 2 to 4 😊

Thirty-six percent of all pizzas ordered in America are pepperoni, making it the poster child for the industry. We've goosed our version with a spicy amatrici sauce—which just might become the new standard.

¼ cup uncooked grits or polenta, for rolling the dough

1 ball prepared pizza dough, at room temperature

2 tablespoons olive oil

1 cup Five-Minute Amatrici-Style Sauce (page 160) or cooked tomato sauce of your choice

4 ounces pepperoni, thinly sliced (ideally from a whole pepperoni)

1 cup grated mozzarella cheese

¼ cup freshly grated Parmigiano-Reggiano cheese

¼ teaspoon red pepper flakes

Kosher salt and freshly ground black pepper to taste

Preheat the grill, roll out and shape the dough, and grill the first side of the crust per the master instructions on page 11 for gas or page 14 for charcoal. Use tongs to transfer it to a peel or rimless baking sheet. Flip the crust to reveal the grilled side.

Spread the entire surface with the sauce. Top with the pepperoni and sprinkle with the cheeses.

Finish grilling the pizza per the master instructions.

Remove from the grill, sprinkle with the red pepper flakes, and season with salt and black pepper. Slice and serve immediately.

ADVENTURE CLUB Replace the pepperoni with your favorite thinly sliced dry-cured salami.

DRINK THIS Merlot is a wine that is as crowd-pleasing as pepperoni. Like the many varieties of pepperoni on the market, merlots range from very simple to mind-blowing.

Mushroom Pizza

Serves 2 to 4

Mushroom purists like their mushroom pizza straight up, while others like it with sausage, pepperoni, onions, or peppers. We say, have it your way.

4   tablespoons olive oil, divided

    Pinch of kosher salt

10 ounces baby bella (baby portabellas) mushrooms, stems trimmed and caps thinly sliced (use an egg slicer for speed and consistency)

¼   cup uncooked grits or polenta, for rolling the dough

1   ball prepared pizza dough, at room temperature

1   cup Crushed Tomato Sauce (page 160)

2   cloves garlic, minced

½   cup grated mozzarella cheese

½   cup grated Asiago cheese

    Leaves from 3 sprigs fresh thyme (about 1 tablespoon) or 2 teaspoons dried

    Freshly ground black pepper to taste

ADVENTURE CLUB Replace the baby bella mushrooms with shiitake, chanterelle, or other wild mushrooms.

DRINK THIS An Oregon Pinot Noir has the perfect earthiness and suppleness to match the flavor and texture of the mushrooms.

If you prefer your mushrooms raw, skip this step. Otherwise, preheat a large, heavy sauté pan over medium heat for 1 to 2 minutes. Add 2 tablespoons of the oil and the salt. When the oil is hot, add the mushrooms and cook, stirring occasionally, until browned, about 10 minutes. Remove from the heat and reserve for topping.

Preheat the grill, roll out and shape the dough, and grill the first side of the crust per the master instructions on page 11 for gas or page 14 for charcoal. Use tongs to transfer it to a peel or rimless baking sheet. Flip the crust to reveal the grilled side.

Spread the entire surface with the sauce, sprinkle with the garlic, and top with the mushrooms. Sprinkle with the cheeses.

Finish grilling the pizza per the master instructions.

Remove from the grill, sprinkle with the thyme, and season with salt and pepper. Slice and serve immediately.

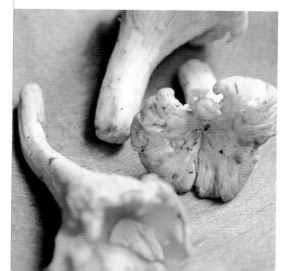

39

Sausage & Sweet Pepper Pizza

Serves 2 to 4

Little Italy's favorite street sandwich—Italian sausage and peppers—comes to life on top of this crispy, smoky pizza crust. This way you get more toppings and less bread. Now that's amore!

1	pound sweet or hot Italian sausage, taken out of the casings, if necessary
¼	cup uncooked grits or polenta, for rolling the dough
1	ball prepared pizza dough, at room temperature
2	tablespoons olive oil
1	cup Tuscan Red Sauce (page 159) or Crushed Tomato Sauce (page 160)
¼	cup pickled sweet and hot peppers, sliced
1	cup grated mozzarella cheese
½	cup grated Monterey Jack cheese
1	teaspoon B&E Sprinkle-icious Spice Blend (page 180) or your favorite spice blend
	Kosher salt and freshly ground black pepper to taste

Place the sausage in a large, heavy skillet. Sauté over medium heat, breaking up any large pieces, until fully cooked. Alternatively, grill the sausage in its casing and slice before using. Drain on paper towels and reserve for topping.

Preheat the grill, roll out and shape the dough, and grill the first side of the crust per the master instructions on page 11 for gas or page 14 for charcoal. Use tongs to transfer it to a peel or rimless baking sheet. Flip the crust to reveal the grilled side.

Spread the entire surface with the sauce. Top with the sausage and peppers, then sprinkle with the cheeses.

Finish grilling the pizza per the master instructions.

Remove from the grill, sprinkle with the spice blend, and season with salt and pepper. Slice and serve immediately.

ADVENTURE CLUB Use piquillo peppers, small, tangy fire-roasted peppers native to the rural village of Lodosa in Navarra, Spain.

DRINK THIS Pick up a six-pack of Peroni® or any other Italian beer.

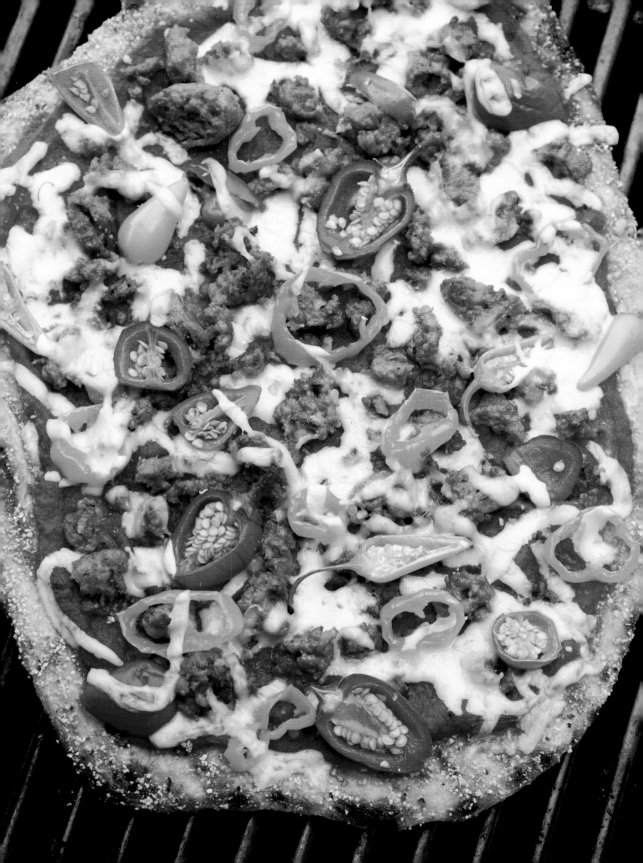

Very Cheesy Pizza

Serves 2 to 4 😊

We've added sharp white Cheddar to the traditional mix to make this the ultimate cheese-lover's pizza.

¼ cup olive oil

10 fresh sage leaves (optional)

½ cup grated mozzarella cheese

½ cup freshly grated Parmigiano-Reggiano cheese

½ cup grated Asiago cheese

½ cup grated sharp white Cheddar cheese

¼ cup uncooked grits or polenta, for rolling the dough

1 ball prepared pizza dough, at room temperature

½ cup Crushed Tomato Sauce (page 160)

Kosher salt and red pepper flakes to taste

ADVENTURE CLUB Replace the four cheeses with Gruyère, aged Cheddar, Gorgonzola, and Romano.

DRINK THIS We like to serve Prosecco, a light, inexpensive sparkling wine from Italy with this pizza. Its crisp acidity is a perfect counterpoint to the richness of the cheeses.

If using the sage, heat the oil in your smallest saucepan over medium heat until it is hot enough to fry the sage. Add the leaves one at a time, taking care that they don't overlap, and fry until rigid and dark green, about 2 minutes. Use a fork to remove them from the oil, set on a paper towel to drain, and reserve for topping. Save 2 tablespoons of your sage-infused oil for brushing the dough.

In a large bowl, mix the four cheeses together. Reserve for topping.

Preheat the grill, roll out and shape the dough, and grill the first side of the crust per the master instructions on page 11 for gas or page 14 for charcoal. Use tongs to transfer it to a peel or rimless baking sheet. Flip the crust to reveal the grilled side.

Spread the entire surface with the sauce and sprinkle with the cheese mixture.

Finish grilling the pizza per the master instructions.

Remove from the grill, garnish with the fried sage, and season with salt and red pepper. Slice and serve immediately.

Presto Pesto Pizza

Serves 2 to 4

Until the 1980s, there were two types of pizza: red and white. Then along came pesto and everything else went green with envy. And for good reason—pesto is rich, intense, and herbaceous. In this classic pesto pizza, the toppings are simple so that the freshness of the sauce shines through.

¼   cup uncooked grits or polenta, for rolling the dough

1   ball prepared pizza dough, at room temperature

2   tablespoons olive oil

1   cup Basil Pesto (page 161) or store-bought

½   cup Tomato-Basil Base (page 159)

8   ounces fresh mozzarella cheese, cut into ¼-inch-thick slices (or 1 cup grated if fresh is unavailable)

2   tablespoons pine nuts

    Kosher salt and freshly ground black pepper to taste

Preheat the grill, roll out and shape the dough, and grill the first side of the crust per the master instructions on page 11 for gas or page 14 for charcoal. Use tongs to transfer it to a peel or rimless baking sheet. Flip the crust to reveal the grilled side.

Spread the entire surface with the pesto. Cover the surface with the tomato-basil base and top with the cheese.

Finish grilling the pizza per the master instructions.

Remove from the grill, garnish with the pine nuts, and season with salt and pepper. Slice and serve immediately.

The Morning After

Bob's favorite morning-after tonic is a slice of leftover pizza, reheated in the toaster oven and topped with a poached or sunny-side-up egg.

ADVENTURE CLUB Replace the basil pesto with pistachio and arugula pesto.

DRINK THIS Pinot Grigio is a light Italian white that brings just the right amount of brightness to balance the pesto.

MARVELOUS & MEATLESS

These pizzas may be meatless, but their hearty flavors will satisfy even the most devoted carnivore.

Fire-Roasted Tomato & Cabrales Pizza

Serves 2 to 4 ⭐

We love all blue cheeses (as you may have noticed), and Cabrales is one of our favorites. Cabrales is a Spanish cheese that has the sharpest, tangiest bite of all the blues. The simple accompanying ingredients in this pizza allow it to sing out loud and proud.

¼   cup uncooked grits or polenta, for rolling the dough

1   ball prepared pizza dough, at room temperature

2   tablespoons olive oil

1   cup Onion Marmalade (page 166)

1¼ cups Fire-Roasted Cherry Tomatoes (page 167)

4   ounces Cabrales or your favorite blue cheese, crumbled

¼   cup pecan pieces, toasted (page 181) and chopped

    Freshly ground black pepper to taste

Preheat the grill, roll out and shape the dough, and grill the first side of the crust per the master instructions on page 11 for gas or page 14 for charcoal. Use tongs to transfer it to a peel or rimless baking sheet. Flip the crust to reveal the grilled side.

Spread the entire surface with the onion marmalade. Top with the tomatoes and sprinkle with the cheese.

Finish grilling the pizza per the master instructions.

Remove the pizza from the grill, garnish with the nuts, and season with pepper. Slice and serve immediately.

ADVENTURE CLUB Replace the cherry tomatoes with heirloom cherry tomatoes.

DRINK THIS Most people think the only thing to drink with a blue cheese is a red wine. We beg to differ. We love a sparkling Spanish Cava with Cabrales—whether it is on its own or melted over our pizza.

Pumpkin-Palooza Pizza

Serves 2 to 4 ⭐

This pizza, inspired by our friend David Sanfield, is a real treat. It's a great way to use fall pumpkins, squash, and greens from farmers' markets. We've upped the ante by adding a few tricks of our own.

1	small sugar pumpkin, Garnet sweet potato, or your favorite squash (try delicata, kobucha, butternut, or acorn)
4	tablespoons salted butter
6	fresh sage leaves
1	bunch chard or other greens, such as kale or spinach
¼	cup uncooked grits or polenta, for rolling the dough
1	ball prepared pizza dough, at room temperature
3	tablespoons olive oil
½	cup Roasted Garlic Paste (page 164)
1	cup shredded Fontina cheese
½	cup shredded mozzarella cheese
3	tablespoons pumpkin seeds (pepitas)
	Kosher salt and freshly ground pepper to taste

Preheat the oven to 400°F.

Cut the pumpkin or squash in half from the stem end. Roast on a sheet pan, cut side down, for 30 minutes. Turn and continue roasting for 30 more minutes, or until the flesh starts to brown (caramelize). Let cool, then scoop out the flesh in small spoonfuls. Reserve 1½ cups and save the rest for an omelet (add bacon and Brie!), or serve as a side dish.

In a small pot over low heat, add the butter and sage leaves. Under a watchful eye, let the butter melt and turn golden brown, about 3 minutes. Remove from the heat. Reserve.

Remove the stems from the chard. Fill a medium pot halfway with water and bring to a boil. Add the greens, then let the water return to a boil. Pour off the water, let the greens cool, and then squeeze out the excess water. Reserve.

Preheat the grill per the master instructions for gas (page 11) or charcoal (page 14). Roll out and shape the dough, transfer to your grilling area, and grill the first side of the crust per the master instructions. When the bottom is marked and browned, use tongs to transfer the crust to a peel or rimless baking sheet. Switch the grill to indirect heat and close the lid to maintain the grill temperature.

Flip the crust to reveal the grilled side. Spread the entire surface with the garlic paste and sprinkle with Fontina. Top with spoonfuls of the pumpkin-squash mixture. Scatter the cooked greens around, separating them so they are evenly distributed. Sprinkle with Mozzarella and pumpkin seeds.

Finish grilling the pizza per the master instructions.

Remove from the grill. Remove the sage from the brown butter (or alternately, crush the leaves and leave them in), then drizzle over top of the pizza. Slice and serve immediately.

ADVENTURE CLUB Drizzle with toasted pumpkin seed oil.

DRINK THIS Hard apple cider is fermented like beer but made from apples. It's crisp and clean and pairs well with pumpkin and greens.

White-on-White Pizza

Serves 2 to 4

This pizza is swaddled in rich white-on-white textures, flavors, and colors. It would be as comfortable in the Museum of Modern Art as it is on your table.

4   tablespoons olive oil, divided

2   cloves garlic, minced

8   spears white asparagus (fresh, canned, or jarred), bottoms peeled with a vegetable peeler if using fresh and cut in half lengthwise

4   oil-packed artichoke hearts (not marinated), cut into eighths

Leaves from 2 sprigs fresh rosemary or 1 teaspoon dried

1   tablespoon fresh lemon juice

¼   cup uncooked grits or polenta, for rolling the dough

1   ball prepared pizza dough, at room temperature

½   cup White Bean Purée (page 162) or store-bought

¼   cup freshly grated Parmigiano-Reggiano cheese

½   cup mascarpone

¼   cup walnut halves, toasted (page 181) and roughly chopped

Kosher salt and freshly ground white pepper to taste

Heat 2 tablespoons of the oil and the garlic together over medium-low heat in a medium sauté pan until the garlic just starts to brown, then add the asparagus, artichokes, rosemary, and lemon juice. Cover and cook for 5 minutes. Remove from the heat and let sit, covered, for 20 minutes. Reserve for topping. Just before using, strain and discard the oil.

Preheat the grill, roll out and shape the dough, and grill the first side of the crust per the master instructions on page 11 for gas or page 14 for charcoal. Use tongs to transfer it to a peel or rimless baking sheet. Flip the crust to reveal the grilled side.

Spread the entire surface with the bean purée. Sprinkle with the Parmigiano. Artfully arrange the artichokes and asparagus on top. Spoon dollops of the mascarpone all around. Finish grilling the pizza per the master instructions.

Remove from the grill, sprinkle the walnuts over all, and season with salt and pepper. Slice and serve immediately.

ADVENTURE CLUB Replace the oil-packed artichoke hearts with braised or steamed fresh hearts.

DRINK THIS Nothing pairs with a white pizza as well as a glass of well-chilled sparkling blanc de blancs.

Tri-Pepper Pizza

Serves 2 to 4

The first taste is with the eyes. This brightly colored pizza is as easy on the eyes as it is pleasing to the palate.

1   red bell pepper

1   orange bell pepper

1   yellow bell pepper

4   tablespoons olive oil, divided

2   tablespoons balsamic vinegar

Kosher salt and freshly ground black pepper to taste

¼   cup uncooked grits or polenta, for rolling the dough

1   ball prepared pizza dough, at room temperature

½   cup Roasted Garlic Paste (page 164)

8   ounces fresh mozzarella cheese, cut into ¼-inch-thick slices (or 1 cup grated if fresh is unavailable)

3   tablespoons Basil Pesto (page 161) or store-bought

ADVENTURE CLUB Top with strips of roasted poblano pepper.

DRINK THIS Barolo is known as the wine of kings and the king of wines. It is made in Italy's Piedmont region—and perhaps that's why it can hold its own with the largesse of balsamic vinegar, which also finds its home there.

Roast the peppers as instructed on page 167, then peel, seed, and cut into strips. In a medium bowl, combine 2 tablespoons of the oil and the vinegar. Add the pepper strips and toss. Season with salt and pepper and let sit for a minimum of 15 minutes or up to a week (refrigerate if longer than 2 hours). Reserve for topping.

Preheat the grill, roll out and shape the dough, and grill the first side of the crust per the master instructions on page 11 for gas or page 14 for charcoal. Use tongs to transfer it to a peel or rimless baking sheet. Flip the crust to reveal the grilled side.

Spread the entire surface with the garlic paste. Top with a tangle of peppers. Place the mozzarella slices over everything.

Finish grilling the pizza per the master instructions.

Remove from the grill and finish by placing a small dollop of pesto on each puddle of mozzarella. Season generously with salt and pepper. Slice and serve immediately.

Blistered Corn, Asparagus & Pesto Pizza

Serves 2 to 4 ⭐

This is Bob's house pizza. The pesto base, sun-dried tomatoes, and Brie smack of an '80s culinary hit parade. But when they share the stage with the blistered corn and grilled asparagus, they create an unmistakably modern taste that is nothing short of addictive.

2   ears corn, husks removed

12   asparagus spears, woody bottoms discarded

4   tablespoons olive oil, divided

Kosher salt to taste

¼   cup uncooked grits or polenta, for rolling the dough

1   ball prepared pizza dough, at room temperature

1   cup Basil Pesto (page 161) or store-bought

12   oil-packed sun-dried tomatoes, cut into 4 strips each

6   ounces Brie, rind removed if preferred, cut into ¼-inch-thick strips, then cut into 1-inch squares

¼   teaspoon red pepper flakes, to taste

Freshly ground black pepper to taste

ADVENTURE CLUB Replace the asparagus with fiddleheads or garlic scapes.

DRINK THIS Cru Beaujolais (such as Moulin-à-Vent, Morgon, and Fleurie) is a poor man's fine burgundy. It is often more supple and made to drink young, making it a perfect complement for a pizza like this that explodes with flavor.

Preheat the grill per the master instructions for gas (page 11) or charcoal (page 14).

Brush the corn and asparagus with 2 tablespoons of the oil and season with salt, then place them on the cooking grate directly over the heat and grill, turning occasionally, until they begin to brown, about 8 minutes. Let cool. To remove the kernels, stand the corn upright. Grip the top of the cob and slide your sharpest knife straight down between the cob and kernels. Cut the asparagus tips off, then cut the remaining stalks into ¼-inch pieces. Reserve both for topping.

Roll out and shape the dough, then grill the first side of the crust per the master instructions. Use tongs to transfer it from the grill to a peel or rimless baking sheet. Flip the crust to reveal the grilled side.

Spread the entire surface with the pesto. Sprinkle with the corn, asparagus, and tomatoes. Top with the cheese.

Finish grilling the pizza per the master instructions.

Remove from the grill, sprinkle with the red pepper, and season with salt and black pepper. Slice and serve immediately.

Magic Mushroom Medley Pizza

Serves 2 to 4 ⭐

Anyone who has ever shared a meal with Elizabeth knows of her obsession with mushrooms. This pizza is a mushroom lover's dream and showcases them with an accent of garlic and cognac, because, in the world according to Elizabeth, less is more.

2 tablespoons unsalted butter

4 tablespoons olive oil, divided

Pinch of kosher salt; more to taste

1 leek, washed well (be fastidious), cut into ¼-inch-thick rounds, and separated into rings

10 ounces mixed wild mushrooms, such as morels, chanterelles, hen of the woods, lobster, king oyster, or other exotic varieties (or reconstituted dried mushrooms), sliced

3 ounces cognac

¼ cup uncooked grits or polenta, for rolling the dough

1 ball prepared pizza dough, at room temperature

½ cup Roasted Garlic Paste (page 164)

6 ounces Camembert cheese, rind removed if preferred, cut into ¼-inch-thick strips

Leaves from 4 sprigs fresh thyme or 2 teaspoons dried

Freshly ground black pepper to taste

ADVENTURE CLUB Shave fresh black truffle over the top of the finished pizza.

DRINK THIS The delicate, earthy tones of the mushroom medley are a natural for the barnyard aromas (and that's a good thing!) of a red burgundy.

Preheat a large sauté pan over medium heat for 1 to 2 minutes. Add the butter and 2 tablespoons of the oil. When the butter bubbles, add a pinch of salt, stir, and add the leeks. Cook for 2 to 3 minutes, then add the mushrooms and cook, stirring occasionally, until browned on the edges, about 10 minutes. Add the cognac, let sit for 5 seconds, then light a long match to it. Stand back and keep wayward clothing and shaggy hair away from the dancing flames. (If you have a gas stove, be aware that spattering particles may cause the alcohol to ignite prematurely.) The flame should burn out after about 10 seconds. If it continues to burn, put it out by placing a lid on the pan. Remove from the heat and reserve for topping.

Preheat the grill, roll out and shape the dough, and grill the first side of the crust per the master instructions on page 11 for gas or page 14 for charcoal. Use tongs to transfer it to a peel or rimless baking sheet. Flip the crust to reveal the grilled side.

Spread the entire surface with the garlic paste, then with the mushroom-leek mixture. Artfully arrange the cheese over the top. Finish grilling the pizza per the master instructions.

Remove from the grill, sprinkle with the thyme, and season generously with salt and pepper. Slice and serve immediately.

Forty Olive & Pimiento Pizza

Serves 2 to 4 ⭐

Pimiento is the Spanish word for a red, heart-shaped sweet pepper. Most of Spain's crop is fire-roasted and either dried and ground into paprika, or stuffed into martini olives. On this olive-lover's pizza, pimientos add color to a savory assortment of green and black olives.

¼ cup walnut pieces, toasted (page 181)

1 ball prepared pizza dough, at room temperature

¼ cup uncooked grits or polenta, for rolling the dough

2 tablespoons olive oil

½ cup Tuscan Red Sauce (page 159) or Crushed Tomato Sauce (page 160)

1½ cups grated manchego cheese

10 Niçoise olives, pitted

10 Kalamata olives, pitted

10 picholine olives, pitted

10 Cerignola olives, pitted

1 small shallot, thinly sliced and separated into rings

¼ cup pimientos or roasted red bell peppers, diced

Zest of 1 lemon, finely grated with a Microplane or zester

Kosher salt and freshly ground black pepper to taste

Knead the walnuts into the dough, cover with plastic wrap, and set aside.

Preheat the grill, roll out and shape the dough, and grill the first side per the master instructions on page 11 for gas or page 14 for charcoal. Use tongs to transfer it to a peel or rimless baking sheet. Flip the crust to reveal the grilled side.

Spread the entire surface with the sauce. Sprinkle with the cheese and top with the olives, shallot rings, and pimientos.

Finish grilling the pizza per the master instructions.

Remove from the grill, sprinkle with the lemon zest, and season with salt and pepper. Slice and serve immediately.

ADVENTURE CLUB Customize the pizza with your own mixture of olives.

DRINK THIS A martini, of course. Is it five o'clock yet?

Fire-Roasted Veggie Pizza

Serves 2 to 4

Grilling vegetables intensifies their flavor and gives them an almost meaty quality, making this a pizza that is guaranteed to appeal to vegetarians, avowed veggie-phobes, and carnivores alike.

1   small red onion, cut into 4 slices

6   tablespoons olive oil, divided

    Kosher salt to taste

2   very large portabella mushrooms, stems removed and caps cut into ½-inch-thick slices

3   Japanese eggplants, cut into ¼-inch-thick slices

1   yellow bell pepper, seeded and quartered

¼   cup uncooked grits or polenta, for rolling the dough

1   ball prepared pizza dough, at room temperature

1   cup Basil or Sun-Dried Tomato Pesto (page 161) or store-bought

20 Fire-Roasted Cherry Tomatoes (page 167)

6   ounces aged goat cheese (chèvre) or Brie, rind removed if preferred, and cut into ¼-inch-thick slices

    B&E Sprinkle-icious Spice Blend (page 180) or your favorite spice blend

    Freshly ground black pepper to taste

ADVENTURE CLUB Add grilled seasonal veggies from your local farmers' market.

DRINK THIS Brew up a pitcher of Red Zinger® ice tea. And if some Southern Comfort® finds its way into it . . . well, that's your business!

Preheat the grill per the master instructions for gas (page 11) or charcoal (page 14).

Soak 4 bamboo skewers in warm water for 10 minutes. Thread each skewer through the center of one onion slice so it resembles a lollipop. Brush them with 1 tablespoon of the oil and season with salt. Brush the mushroom and eggplant slices and bell pepper on both sides with 3 tablespoons of the oil and season with salt.

Place the onions, mushrooms, eggplant, and bell pepper on the cooking grate directly over the heat and grill until well marked and tender, about 4 minutes per side. Let cool, then slice the bell pepper into thin strips, pull the skewers out of the onions, and separate into rings. Reserve for topping.

Roll out and shape the dough, then grill the first side of the crust per the master instructions. Use tongs to transfer it from the grill to a peel or rimless baking sheet. Flip the crust to reveal the grilled side.

Spread the surface with the pesto and artfully arrange the grilled veggies and tomatoes over the top. Sprinkle with the cheese.

Finish grilling the pizza per the master instructions.

Remove from the grill and season with the spice blend, salt, and pepper. Slice and serve immediately.

Lucy in the Sky with Pizza

Serves 2 to 4

This pizza is a psychedelic assemblage of bright colors and fresh, flavorful vegetables.
Timothy Leary, R.I.P.

8   spears asparagus, woody bottoms removed

3   tablespoons olive oil, divided

     Kosher salt to taste

¼   cup uncooked grits or polenta, for rolling the dough

1   ball prepared pizza dough, at room temperature

¼   cup Sun-Dried Tomato Pesto (page 161) or store-bought

1   orange bell pepper, seeded and cut into thin rings

12   yellow cherry tomatoes, cut in half

12   cured black olives, pitted

12   cloves garlic, roasted (page 164)

8   ounces Brie, rind removed if preferred, and sliced

2   tablespoons chopped mixed fresh herbs, such as basil, mint, or tarragon

     Freshly ground black pepper to taste

Preheat the grill per the master instructions for gas (page 11) or charcoal (page 14).

Brush the asparagus with 1 tablespoon of the oil and season with salt, then place it on the cooking grate directly over the heat and grill, turning occasionally, until it begins to brown, about 8 minutes. Let cool and reserve for topping.

Roll out and shape the dough, then grill the first side of the crust per the master instructions. Use tongs to transfer it from the grill to a peel or rimless baking sheet. Flip the crust to reveal the grilled side.

Spread the entire surface with the pesto. Top with pepper rings, tomatoes, olives, garlic, and asparagus. Artfully place the cheese on top.

Finish grilling the pizza per the master instructions.

Remove from the grill, sprinkle with the herbs, and season with salt and pepper. Slice and serve immediately.

ADVENTURE CLUB Replace the Brie with Chèvre Noir, a two-year-old aged goat milk Cheddar.

DRINK THIS Australian Sauvignon Blancs are juicy and fruity. The great ones display notes of ripe peaches, apricots, and passion fruit, making them a perfect pairing for our psychedelic pizza.

Plan for Grilled-Overs

Elizabeth´s time-saving trick for making pizzas that include precooked ingredients is to grill extra so that it is ready to slice and use on a pizza the next day. Affectionately referred to as grilled-overs, most of these can be refrigerated for up to 3 days.

SEAWORTHY PIZZAS

Seafood adds an unexpected bite to the pizza experience. In this section we have riffed on some of America's favorite dishes to create pizzas that are swimmingly delicious.

Maine Event Lobster & Corn Pizza

Serves 2 to 4 ⭐

The rich and decadent ingredients assembled here create a luxurious pizza that Donald Trump would be proud to serve at his Fourth of July party. If you can't find lobster in your market, buy frozen cooked crayfish; it makes a tasty and economical substitute.

2	ears corn, husked
3	tablespoons olive oil, divided
	Kosher salt to taste
¼	cup (½ stick) unsalted butter
1	cup Tuscan Red Sauce (page 159) or Crushed Tomato Sauce (page 160)
2	tablespoons crème fraîche or sour cream
¼	cup uncooked grits or polenta, for rolling the dough
1	ball prepared pizza dough, at room temperature
4	ounces St. André cheese (a triple crème cheese)
1	cup cooked lobster meat
4	fresh chives, thinly sliced
	Freshly ground black pepper to taste

ADVENTURE CLUB Grill your own lobster.

DRINK THIS You know, the Don would serve nothing less than pink Champagne from France.

Preheat the grill per the master instructions for gas (page 11) or charcoal (page 14).

Brush the corn with 1 tablespoon of the oil and season with salt, then place on the cooking grate directly over the heat and grill, turning occasionally, until it begins to brown, about 8 minutes. Let cool. Remove the kernels from the cob. Reserve for topping.

Just before making the pizza, in a small saucepan over medium heat (or on the grill), melt the butter. Reduce the heat to low or set it off to the side of the grill.

In a medium bowl, combine the tomato sauce and crème fraîche.

Roll out and shape the dough, then grill the first side of the crust per the master instructions. Use tongs to transfer it from the grill to a peel or rimless baking sheet. Flip the crust to reveal the grilled side.

Spread the entire surface with the sauce. Top with the corn and cheese.

Finish grilling the pizza per the master instructions.

While the pizza finishes cooking, add the lobster meat to the butter. Cover and warm for 3 minutes, then remove from the heat. When the pizza is hot off the grill, arrange the lobster on top. Sprinkle with the chives and season with salt and pepper. Slice and serve immediately.

Drunken Shrimp Pizza

Serves 2 to 4

Even cardboard would taste good if it were pickled in pepper vodka, seasoned with garlic, slathered in olive oil, and topped with creamy mozzarella. Put it all on a pizza crust and it's heaven.

1	pound colossal shrimp, thawed if necessary, shelled, and deveined
1	cup pepper vodka, or 1 cup vodka plus 1 teaspoon Tabasco sauce
4	cloves garlic, minced
6	tablespoons olive oil, divided
	Kosher salt to taste
¼	cup uncooked grits or polenta, for rolling the dough
1	ball prepared pizza dough, at room temperature
1	cup Five-Minute Amatrici-Style Sauce (page 160) or other cooked tomato sauce
8	ounces fresh mozzarella cheese, cut into ¼-inch-thick slices (or 1 cup grated if fresh is unavailable)
10	black olives, such as Niçoise or Kalamata, pitted
	Zest of 1 lemon, finely grated with a Microplane or a zester
	Freshly ground black pepper to taste

ADVENTURE CLUB Substitute crawfish tails for the shrimp.

DRINK THIS Hey, isn't that a bottle of pepper vodka over there?!

Pat the shrimp dry. Combine the vodka, garlic, and 4 tablespoons of the oil in a large nonreactive metal or glass bowl. Add the shrimp, cover with plastic wrap, and let marinate in the refrigerator for 30 minutes.

Preheat the grill per the master instructions for gas (page 11) or charcoal (page 14).

Remove the shrimp from the marinade and season with salt. Place them on the cooking grate directly over the heat and grill until no longer translucent, 2 to 3 minutes per side. Reserve for topping.

Roll out and shape the dough, then grill the first side of the crust per the master instructions. Use tongs to transfer it from the grill to a peel or rimless baking sheet. Flip the crust to reveal the grilled side.

Spread the entire surface with the sauce. Artfully arrange the mozzarella slices, then the shrimp and olives on top.

Finish grilling the pizza per the master instructions.

Remove from the grill, sprinkle with the lemon zest, and season with salt and pepper. Slice and serve immediately.

Clams Casino Pizza

Serves 2 to 4

Odds are that bacon, garlic, white wine, and clams will be a winning bet in any house.

5   strips bacon, chopped

¼   cup (½ stick) unsalted butter

5   cloves garlic, minced

⅓   cup white wine

18 fresh clams in the shell

½   cup ricotta cheese

½   cup boursin or other soft garlic cheese
    (one 5.2-ounce round)

2   slices stale white bread, grated, or
    ⅓ cup plain breadcrumbs

¼   cup uncooked grits or polenta, for rolling
    the dough

1   ball prepared pizza dough, at room
    temperature

2   tablespoons olive oil

2   tablespoons freshly grated Parmigiano-
    Reggiano cheese

2   tablespoons grated pecorino cheese

    Kosher salt and freshly ground black pepper
    to taste

ADVENTURE CLUB Turn your Clams Casino into a Manhattan Clam Pizza by replacing the bacon with ¼ cup diced Spanish chorizo and substituting Five-Minute Amatrici-Style Sauce (page 160) for the ricotta-boursin sauce.

DRINK THIS Chablis is a region in Burgundy that produces crisp, minerally Chardonnays. This wine won't overpower the delicate flavor of the clams as an oakier California Chardonnay might.

Preheat a heavy sauté pan over medium heat for 1 to 2 minutes. Add the bacon and cook, stirring, until the fat begins to render. Add the butter and garlic; cook just until the butter is melted and bubbling. Remove 1 tablespoon of the garlic butter to a bowl. Add the wine to the pan, stir, and simmer for 2 minutes. Remove from the heat.

Fill a large pot with 3 inches of water and bring to a boil. Just before making the pizza, add the clams and cover. Boil until the clams open, 5 to 7 minutes. Remove from the heat and take the clams out of their shells. Discard unopened clams.

In a medium bowl, use a fork to mix together the ricotta and boursin. Reserve for topping.

Mix the grated bread into the reserved garlic butter. Place the bread crumbs on a cookie sheet and toast in a preheated 300ºF oven for 10 minutes. Let cool and set aside.

Preheat the grill, roll out and shape the dough, and grill the first side of the crust per the master instructions on page 11 for gas or page 14 for charcoal. Transfer it to a peel or rimless baking sheet. Flip the crust to reveal the grilled side.

Spread the entire surface with ricotta sauce. Arrange the clams on top and sprinkle with the bacon mixture. Sprinkle the cheeses over all.

Finish grilling the pizza per the master instructions.

Remove from the grill, sprinkle with the breadcrumbs, and season with salt and pepper. Slice and serve immediately.

Smokin´ Salmon Pizza

Serves 2 to 4

This is the perfect recipe to initiate yourself into the world of grilled pizza. Since the only thing you need to grill is the crust, there is only one step to focus on. All the toppings are added after the crust has finished cooking. The result is deceptively fancy and luxurious—not a surprise if you consider that the toppings are a take on the well-loved smoked salmon canapé.

¼ cup uncooked grits or polenta, for rolling the dough

1 ball prepared pizza dough, at room temperature

2 tablespoons olive oil

½ cup boursin or other soft garlic cheese (one 5.2-ounce round)

1 small shallot, minced

4 slices smoked salmon (about 4 ounces), cut into strips

Zest of 1 lemon, finely grated with a Microplane or a zester

2 tablespoons chopped fresh dill or chives

Freshly ground black pepper to taste

Preheat the grill, roll out and shape the dough, and grill the first side of the crust per the master instructions on page 11 for gas or page 14 for charcoal. Flip the crust and grill until the second side is well browned, 2 to 3 minutes. (Since you're not melting cheese or warming any toppings, you don't need to switch to indirect heat for a gas grill.)

Remove from the grill and immediately spread the entire surface with the boursin. Sprinkle with the shallot and top with the strips of salmon. Finish with the zest, dill, and pepper. Slice and serve immediately.

ADVENTURE CLUB Replace the salmon with pieces of smoked sturgeon.

DRINK THIS Smoked salmon and champagne are an unbeatable combination.

Appetizer Math

Grilled pizza makes a fabulous appetizer for any dinner party (whether or not another pizza is the main course). Plan on one to two slices per person, but be prepared for your guests to revolt until they get more.

PuTTANesCA

Puttanesca Pizza

Serves 2 to 4

This is based on the classic Italian recipe for "whore's pasta"—so called because it's cheap, quick, and easy.

¼ cup uncooked grits or polenta, for rolling the dough

1 ball prepared pizza dough, at room temperature

2 tablespoons olive oil

1 cup Five-Minute Amatrici-Style Sauce (page 160)

2 cloves garlic, minced

½ cup Niçoise olives, drained and pitted

1 tablespoon capers, drained and patted dry

¼ cup grated pecorino romano cheese

1 cup grated Asiago cheese

6 anchovy fillets

B&E Drizzle-icious Infused Oil (page 180) or your favorite flavored oil

Preheat the grill, roll out and shape the dough, and grill the first side of the crust per the master instructions on page 11 for gas or page 14 for charcoal. Use tongs to transfer it to a peel or rimless baking sheet. Flip the crust to reveal the grilled side.

Spread the entire surface with the sauce. Sprinkle with the garlic, olives, and capers, then with the cheeses. Artfully place the anchovies on top.

Finish grilling the pizza per the master instructions.

Remove from the grill and drizzle with the infused oil to taste. Slice and serve immediately.

ADVENTURE CLUB Replace the anchovies with white anchovies, available in specialty food stores.

DRINK THIS You need a rough, earthy wine like a Malbec from Chile to stand up to the pungent, unrefined flavors in this pizza.

Crab & Artichoke Pizza

Serves 2 to 4

Crabmeat and artichokes are a classic pairing. When it comes to shopping for crab, there are three forms to choose from. The snowy white jumbo lump crabmeat comes from the largest crabs and is the most expensive. Backfin comes from the back and the belly, and the best quality is sold in the refrigerated section of your fish department. The pinkish colored claw meat is usually canned and can be found in the aisle alongside canned tuna. Any of these will work beautifully on this pizza.

¼   cup uncooked grits or polenta, for rolling the dough

1   ball prepared pizza dough, at room temperature

2   tablespoons olive oil

1   cup Artichoke Spread (page 163) or store-bought (sometimes sold as artichoke pesto)

1   cup crabmeat, picked over for shells and cartilage

12   Fire-Roasted Cherry Tomatoes (page 167)

¼   cup freshly grated pecorino romano cheese

Leaves from 2 sprigs fresh tarragon

Kosher salt and freshly ground black pepper to taste

Preheat the grill, roll out and shape the dough, and grill the first side of the crust per the master instructions on page 11 for gas or page 14 for charcoal. Use tongs to transfer it to a peel or rimless baking sheet. Flip the crust to reveal the grilled side.

Spread the entire surface with the artichoke spread. Top with the crabmeat and tomatoes and sprinkle with the cheese.

Finish grilling the pizza per the master instructions.

Remove from the grill, sprinkle with the tarragon, and season with salt and pepper. Slice and serve immediately.

ADVENTURE CLUB Use Alaskan king crab.

DRINK THIS New Zealand Sauvignon Blancs are known for their crisp, clean, grassy, citrusy notes, and they are a perfect match for the delicate flavors of the crab and artichoke.

PORKILICIOUS PIZZAS

If it looks like pork, smells like pork, or tastes like pork, it's great on a pizza. These are our favorite porky pies.

Grilled Pineapple & Pancetta Pizza

Serves 2 to 4 ⭐

The combo of pineapple and ham is an all-time classic and perfect on a pizza. Here, we've grilled fresh pineapple to accentuate its sweetness, and upped the ante by substituting Italian pancetta for Canadian bacon.

4 ounces pancetta, sliced ¼ inch thick, or slab bacon, diced

1 ripe, fresh pineapple, peeled, cored, and cut into ½-inch-thick rings

1 tablespoon nut oil or vegetable oil

2 tablespoons sugar

6 scallions, root ends trimmed

3 tablespoons olive oil, divided

Kosher salt to taste; more to taste

¼ cup uncooked grits or polenta, for rolling the dough

1 ball prepared pizza dough, at room temperature

½ cup Onion Marmalade (page 166)

6 ounces Camembert cheese, sliced

2 tablespoons flaked sweetened coconut, toasted (page 181)

Red pepper flakes to taste

ADVENTURE CLUB Replace the pancetta with barbecued pork belly.

DRINK THIS Satisfy your inner child with an adult version of Hawaiian Punch®. Mix together a splash of pineapple juice, 1 cup orange juice (ideally fresh), the juice of 1 lime, a splash of grenadine, a splash of Grand Marnier®, and a shot or two of white rum. Shake over ice and serve.

Cook the pancetta or bacon in a small skillet over medium-high heat until crispy, and drain on a paper towel. Reserve for topping.

Preheat the grill per the master instructions for gas (page 11) or charcoal (page 14).

Brush the pineapple rings with the nut oil, sprinkle both sides with the sugar, and let sit for 5 minutes. Brush the scallions with a little of the olive oil and sprinkle with salt. Place the pineapple and scallions on the cooking grate directly over the heat and grill until the pineapple is well marked and the scallions are limp and charred in spots, 3 to 5 minutes per side. Remove from the grill. Chop the scallions. Reserve for topping.

Roll out and shape the dough, then grill the first side of the crust per the master instructions. Use tongs to transfer it from the grill to a peel or rimless baking sheet. Flip the crust to reveal the grilled side.

Spread the entire surface with the marmalade. Top with the cheese. Artfully arrange the pineapple rings on top. Sprinkle with the pancetta and scallions.

Finish grilling the pizza per the master instructions.

Remove from the grill, sprinkle with the toasted coconut, and season with salt and red pepper. Slice and serve immediately.

Prosciutto & Parmigiano Pizza

Serves 2 to 4

Prosciutto and Parmigiano-Reggiano go together like Romeo and Juliet. That's not surprising since they both come from Parma, a small town in Italy's Po Valley, south of Milan. The pigs are fattened with the whey (a by-product of the cheese-making process) from the Parmigiano, resulting in a buttery and distinctive tasting air-cured ham. Parmigiano is the godfather of all Parmesan cheese. It is made from the milk of free-roaming Holstein-Friesians cows and aged in vaults for a minimum of two years, resulting in a rich and nutty texture. Both are expensive, but worth every euro.

10	spears asparagus, woody bottoms removed
3	tablespoons olive oil, divided
	Kosher salt to taste
¼	cup uncooked grits or polenta, for rolling the dough
1	ball prepared pizza dough, at room temperature
½	cup Roasted Garlic Paste (page 164)
½	cup freshly grated Parmigiano-Reggiano cheese
8	ounces fresh mozzarella cheese, cut into ¼-inch-thick slices (or 1 cup grated if fresh is unavailable)
20	Fire-Roasted Cherry Tomatoes (page 167)
8	thin slices prosciutto, cut into ¼-inch-wide ribbons
	B&E Drizzle-icious Infused Oil (page 180) or favorite flavored oil
	Freshly ground black pepper to taste

Preheat the grill per the master instructions for gas (page 11) or charcoal (page 14).

Brush the asparagus with 1 tablespoon of the oil and season with salt, then place on the cooking grate directly over the heat and grill, turning occasionally, until the spears begin to brown in spots, about 8 minutes. Let cool and reserve for topping.

Roll out and shape the dough, then grill the first side of the crust per the master instructions. Use tongs to transfer it from the grill to a peel or rimless baking sheet. Flip the crust to reveal the grilled side. Spread the entire surface with the garlic paste. Sprinkle with the Parmigiano and top with mozzarella, asparagus, and tomatoes. Finish grilling the pizza per the master instructions.

Remove from the grill, scatter the prosciutto about, and drizzle with the infused oil. Season with salt and pepper. Slice and serve immediately.

ADVENTURE CLUB Replace the prosciutto with lardo—a unique Italian specialty made from the layer of fat found directly under the pig's skin. Mario Batali refers to it affectionately as "prosciutto blanco."

DRINK THIS Concoct an effervescent lemon drop by mixing Lemonata (a carbonated lemon beverage made by San Pellegrino®) with vodka. Garnish with a lemon slice.

White Bean, Italian Sausage & Rapini Pizza

Serves 2 to 4

This is everything you could hope for in a rustic Tuscan dinner. As we like to say, bean there, sausage that.

4	tablespoons olive oil, divided
1	bunch rapini (broccoli rabe), ends trimmed
2	cloves garlic, minced
¼	teaspoon red pepper flakes
2	hot or sweet Italian sausages
¼	cup uncooked grits or polenta, for rolling the dough
1	ball prepared pizza dough, at room temperature
½	cup White Bean Purée (page 162) or store-bought
¼	cup grated pecorino romano cheese
½	cup grated mozzarella cheese
	Zest of 1 lemon, finely grated with a Microplane or zester
	Kosher salt and freshly ground black pepper to taste

ADVENTURE CLUB Make your own Italian sausage or experiment with different handmade fresh sausage from an Italian grocery.

DRINK THIS This pizza may be rustic in style, but we like to go all out with the wine and pour a so-called Super Tuscan—the superhero of Italian wines.

Preheat a large, heavy sauté pan over medium heat. Add 2 tablespoons of the oil and the rapini and cook until it turns bright green and starts to soften, 2 to 3 minutes. Add the garlic and red pepper; stir well to coat. Cover and continue to cook until the rapini is cooked through, about 5 minutes. Reserve for topping.

Preheat the grill per the master instructions for gas (page 11) or charcoal (page 14).

Prick the sausages with a toothpick several times to prevent unwanted explosions. Place the sausages on the cooking grate over indirect heat. Grill, turning occasionally, until cooked through, about 20 minutes. Let cool. Cut into ¼-inch-thick rounds just before topping.

Roll out and shape the dough, then grill the first side of the crust per the master instructions. Use tongs to transfer it from the grill to a peel or rimless baking sheet. Flip the crust to reveal the grilled side.

Spread the entire surface with the bean purée. Top with the rapini and sausage. Sprinkle with the cheeses.

Finish grilling the pizza per the master instructions.

Remove from the grill, sprinkle with the lemon zest, and season with salt and black pepper. Slice and serve immediately.

B•BLT Pizza

Serves 2 to 4

One of our favorite salads is the BLT-inspired grilled hearts of romaine topped with bacon, tomatoes, and a luscious homemade blue cheese dressing. Here we add a crispy crust and the salad becomes a meal.

1	heart of romaine lettuce or 1 head of romaine stripped down to the heart
3	tablespoons olive oil, divided
	Kosher salt to taste
¼	cup uncooked grits or polenta, for rolling the dough
1	ball prepared pizza dough, at room temperature
	Drizzle of B&E Drizzle-icious Infused Oil (page 180)
1	cup Tomato-Basil Base (page 159)
8	strips center-cut bacon, cooked until crisp, then crumbled
6	ounces Saga or other blue cheese, crumbled
	Freshly ground black pepper to taste

ADVENTURE CLUB Join the Bacon-of-the-Month Club (www.gratefulpalate.com) and replace your bacon with one of their artisanal bacons or Schaller & Weber® double-smoked bacon.

DRINK THIS We're reaching down under for this one and choosing Australia's most popular grape: Shiraz. Its full fruit and luscious quality make it a great match for the smoky bacon and grilled lettuce.

Preheat the grill per the master instructions for gas (page 11) or charcoal (page 14).

Cut the romaine heart in half lengthwise, keeping the core intact. Brush with 1 tablespoon of the olive oil and season with salt. Place on the cooking grate directly over the heat. Grill until the outer leaves are charred but the inside is still crisp, 2 to 3 minutes per side. Let cool, then cut and discard the core and slice crosswise into ½-inch-wide ribbons. Reserve for topping.

Roll out and shape the dough, then grill the first side of the crust per the master instructions. Use tongs to transfer it from the grill to a peel or rimless baking sheet. Flip the crust to reveal the grilled side.

Drizzle the entire surface with the infused oil, then top with the tomato sauce. Sprinkle with the bacon and cheese.

Finish grilling the pizza per the master instructions.

Remove from the grill, top with the romaine, and season with salt and pepper. Slice and serve immediately.

Croque Monsieur Pizza

Serves 2 to 4

Every self-respecting bistro in France serves a Croque Monsieur—their version of a gourmet ham and cheese sandwich. We've taken the same ingredients and placed them on a crispy crust to deliver a pizza that is nothing short of *magnifique*.

¼   cup grated mozzarella cheese

½   cup grated Gruyère or Comté cheese

¼   cup freshly grated Parmigiano-Reggiano cheese

½   cup Roasted Garlic Paste (page 164)

1   tablespoon strong Dijon mustard

¼   cup uncooked grits or polenta, for rolling the dough

1   ball prepared pizza dough, at room temperature

2   tablespoons olive oil

6   ounces sliced cooked (not cured) ham, julienned (cut into ¼-inch-wide strips)

10 cornichons (miniature French-style gherkins), cut in half lengthwise

    Kosher salt and freshly ground black pepper to taste

In a medium bowl, combine the three cheeses. In a small bowl, mix together the garlic paste and mustard. Reserve both for topping.

Preheat the grill, roll out and shape the dough, and grill the first side of the crust per the master instructions on page 11 for gas or page 14 for charcoal. Use tongs to transfer it to a peel or rimless baking sheet. Flip the crust to reveal the grilled side.

Spread the entire surface with the garlic-mustard paste. Top with the ham and sprinkle with the cheese mixture.

Finish grilling the pizza per the master instructions.

Remove from the grill, place the cornichons, cut side down, artfully around the surface, and season with salt and pepper. Slice and serve immediately.

ADVENTURE CLUB Replace the cooked ham with jambon de bayonne, a French-style prosciutto.

DRINK THIS Pretend you are in a French café and serve with a hard sparkling apple or pear cider.

Queso Fundido Pizza

Serves 2 to 4

Everyone's favorite cheesy Mexican appetizer can now be one of your favorite pizzas.

1   pound raw Mexican chorizo sausage or any hot, spicy pork sausage, casings removed

¼   cup uncooked grits or polenta, for rolling the dough

1   ball prepared pizza dough, at room temperature

2   tablespoons olive oil

¼   cup adobo sauce (from a can of chipotles in adobo sauce)

1½ cups grated Chihuahua or Monterey Jack cheese

¼   cup crumbled queso fresco cheese

1   large poblano pepper, roasted (page 167), or canned green chile

2   plum tomatoes, diced

1   ripe avocado, peeled, pitted, and cut into thin wedges

    Kosher salt and freshly ground black pepper to taste

Preheat a small sauté pan over medium-high heat for 1 to 2 minutes. Add the sausage and cook, stirring occasionally and breaking up any clumps, until no longer pink. Drain on paper towels and reserve for topping.

Preheat the grill, roll out and shape the dough, and grill the first side of the crust per the master instructions on page 11 for gas or page 14 for charcoal. Use tongs to transfer it to a peel or rimless baking sheet. Flip the crust to reveal the grilled side.

Spread the entire surface with the adobo sauce. Top with the cheeses. Sprinkle with the crumbled chorizo, poblano strips, and tomatoes.

Finish grilling the pizza per the master instructions.

Remove from the grill, garnish with the avocado, and season with salt and pepper. Slice and serve immediately.

ADVENTURE CLUB Slice as many chipotles as you dare and sprinkle them over the pizza.

DRINK THIS When in a Mexican state of mind, do what the Mexicans do and pop open a bottle of Negra Modelo or other Mexican beer.

Yukon Gold Rush Pizza

Serves 2 to 4 ☆

Potatoes don't instantly come to mind when you think of common pizza toppings. But this pizza is anything but common. We've riffed off the classic French *tarte aux pommes de terre* for a creation that is pure gold.

4   medium Yukon Gold potatoes, left unpeeled and cut into ⅛-inch-thick rounds

4   tablespoons olive oil, divided

     Kosher salt

4   ounces thickly sliced pancetta, diced

¼   cup uncooked grits or polenta, for rolling the dough

1   ball prepared pizza dough, at room temperature

½   cup Roasted Garlic Paste (page 164)

1½   cups grated Gruyère cheese

¼   cup Niçoise olives, drained and pitted

     Leaves from 2 sprigs fresh rosemary or 2 teaspoons dried

     B&E Drizzle-icious Infused Oil (page 180) or favorite flavored oil

     Freshly ground black pepper

ADVENTURE CLUB For a completely different tuber experience, use sweet potatoes (ideally the Garnet variety).

DRINK THIS A white Burgundy (made in France from the chardonnay grape) will make this monsieur very happy.

Preheat the grill per the master instructions for gas (page 11) or charcoal (page 14).

Brush the sliced potatoes with 2 tablespoons of the oil and season with salt. Place them on the cooking grate over indirect heat, and grill until well marked and cooked through, about 20 minutes (or bake on a sheet pan in a preheated 350°F oven), turning them once. Reserve for topping.

Meanwhile, preheat a medium, heavy sauté pan over medium-high heat for 1 to 2 minutes, then fry the pancetta, stirring, until crisp. Reserve for topping.

Roll out and shape the dough, then grill the first side of the crust per the master instructions. Use tongs to transfer it from the grill to a peel or rimless baking sheet. Flip the crust to reveal the grilled side.

Spread the entire surface with the garlic paste and sprinkle with half the cheese. Cover with the potato slices, placing them edge to edge. Sprinkle with the pancetta and the remaining cheese. Artfully arrange the olives and rosemary over the top.

Finish grilling the pizza per the master instructions.

Remove from the grill. Finish with a drizzle of the infused oil and season with salt and pepper. Slice and serve immediately.

Fennelicious Pizza

Serves 2 to 4

Fennel is a highly aromatic bulbous vegetable that tastes like a cross between celery and licorice. It is heralded for its flavor as well as its health benefits. We can't decide if we are more excited about this pizza because it tastes delicious or because it's good for us.

1   fennel bulb, trimmed and cut lengthwise into 4 even slices (reserve the fennel fronds)

3   tablespoons olive oil, divided

Kosher salt to taste

2   sweet Italian sausages with fennel seeds

¼   cup uncooked grits or polenta, for rolling the dough

2   tablespoons fennel seeds

1   ball prepared pizza dough, at room temperature

½   cup Tuscan Red Sauce (page 159)

½   cup Onion Marmalade (page 166)

1   cup sliced Taleggio or Fontina cheese

Freshly ground black pepper to taste

ADVENTURE CLUB Sip on a sambuca while grilling your pizza.

DRINK THIS Rosés have gotten a bad rap. Chilled, crisp, and clean tasting, we love them paired with pizza and just about anything else in the summertime. The most famous rosés come from the south of France, but these days most wine regions produce good-value versions.

Preheat the grill per the master instructions for gas (page 11) or charcoal (page 14).

Brush the fennel slices with 1 tablespoon of the oil and season with salt. Chop 2 tablespoons of the reserved fennel fronds. Poke the sausages with a toothpick in several places (to keep them from exploding). Place the fennel and sausages on the cooking grate directly over the heat and grill until well marked and cooked through, about 25 minutes, turning occasionally. Let cool, then cut out and discard the core of the fennel and separate into pieces. Cut the sausages into ¼-inch-thick rounds. Reserve for topping.

Knead the fennel seeds into the dough. Roll out and shape the dough, then grill the first side of the crust per the master instructions. Use tongs to transfer it from the grill to a peel or rimless baking sheet. Flip the crust to reveal the grilled side.

Spread the entire surface with the sauce, then the marmalade. Top with the fennel and sausage and sprinkle with the cheese.

Finish grilling the pizza per the master instructions.

Remove from the grill, sprinkle with the chopped fennel fronds, and season with salt and pepper. Slice and serve immediately.

Spanish Fly Pizza

Serves 2 to 4

We've taken all our favorite Spanish tapas and combined them into one seductive pizza. *Olé!*

¼ cup uncooked grits or polenta, for rolling the dough

1 ball prepared pizza dough, at room temperature

2 tablespoons olive oil

½ cup Onion Marmalade (page 166)

4 ounces Spanish chorizo, very thinly sliced

1½ cups grated Manchego cheese

6 ounces quince paste, cut into ½-inch cubes

Smoked Spanish paprika (pimentón) to taste

Kosher salt and freshly ground black pepper to taste

ADVENTURE CLUB Top the finished pizza with ¼ cup salted, roasted Marcona almonds.

DRINK THIS We love Spanish Rioja with this pizza. Our favorites are made entirely from Tempranillo grapes.

Preheat the grill, roll out and shape the dough, and grill the first side of the crust per the master instructions on page 11 for gas or page 14 for charcoal. Use tongs to transfer it to a peel or rimless baking sheet. Flip the crust to reveal the grilled side.

Spread the entire surface with the marmalade. Top with the chorizo, cheese, and quince paste cubes.

Finish grilling the pizza per the master instructions.

Remove from the grill, finish with a dusting of paprika, and season with salt and pepper. Slice and serve immediately.

Note: Look for quince paste and Manchego cheese in specialty cheese and gourmet stores. Manchego is Spain's famous sheep's milk cheese.

Pimiento Cheese Pizza

Serves 2 to 4 ✕

What is sometimes referred to as "the paté of the South" has taken the nation by storm! To truly respect its origins, you should make the pimiento cheese from scratch.

¼   cup uncooked grits or polenta, for rolling the dough

1   ball prepared pizza dough, at room temperature

3   tablespoons olive oil

1½   cups Pimiento Cheese (page 175)

3   tomatoes, ideally heirloom, sliced into ¼-inch slices

6   strips bacon (we love Nueske's®!), sliced crosswise into ¼-inch strips and fried until crispy

¼   cup inner celery leaves, separated and chopped

    Kosher salt and freshly ground black pepper

ADVENTURE CLUB Roast your own pimientos.

DRINK THIS Sweet tea vodka is the alcoholic version of ice tea. Serve your favorite brand over ice and garnish with a twist of orange.

Preheat the grill per the master instructions for gas (page 11) or charcoal (page 14). Roll out and shape the dough, transfer to your grilling area, and grill the first side of the crust per the master instructions. When the bottom is marked and browned, use tongs to transfer the crust to a peel or rimless baking sheet. Switch the grill to indirect heat and close the lid to maintain the grill temperature.

Flip the crust to reveal the grilled side. Spread with the pimiento mixture, then top with the tomato slices and bacon.

Finish grilling the pizza per the master instructions.

Remove from the grill, sprinkle with the chopped celery leaves, and season with salt and pepper. Slice and serve immediately.

Greens on White Pizza

Serves 2 to 4 ⭐ 🍴

Pizzeria Bianco in Scottsdale, Arizona, is one of our favorite pizzerias in America. Chef-owner Chris Bianco loves pizza-making so much that he kisses every pie before placing it in his wood-burning brick oven. Chris's menu offers only six varieties, and none of his pizzas have more than four toppings. We fell in love with the simple peppery arugula-topped three-cheese pizza he calls Biancoverde Pizza. This is our homage to it.

¼ cup uncooked grits or polenta, for rolling the dough

1 ball prepared pizza dough, at room temperature

2 tablespoons olive oil, plus extra to drizzle on the arugula

½ cup Roasted Garlic Paste (page 164)

⅔ cup grated mozzarella cheese

⅔ cup grated Asiago cheese

⅔ cup ricotta cheese

1-2 teaspoons white truffle oil

1 cup fresh arugula (ideally baby arugula)

4 ounces thinly sliced prosciutto

Fleur de sel or kosher salt and freshly ground black pepper to taste

Preheat the grill, roll out and shape the dough, and grill the first side of the crust per the master instructions on page 11 for gas or page 14 for charcoal. Use tongs to transfer it to a peel or rimless baking sheet. Flip the crust to reveal the grilled side.

Spread the entire surface with the garlic paste, then top with the mozzarella and Asiago, and spoon dollops of the ricotta over all.

Finish grilling the pizza per the master instructions.

Remove from the grill and drizzle with some of the truffle oil. Drizzle the arugula lightly with olive oil and toss, then place immediately on top of pizza (so that the heat of the pizza wilts it). Arrange the prosciutto on top and season with salt and pepper. Slice and serve immediately.

ADVENTURE CLUB Replace the truffle oil with shaved white truffles.

DRINK THIS Make yourself a Tangerita by mixing 2 ounces tequila, 2 ounces fresh lime juice, 1 ounce of Triple Sec, and 4 ounces fresh tangerine juice. Shake over ice and serve.

Country Ham & Fig Pizza

Serves 2 to 4 ☆

Country ham is a mainstay of the southern table and is sometimes referred to as America's prosciutto. The salty, meaty ham is best sliced thin and is frequently served on biscuits—and in Elizabeth's home with fig jam. Add dollops of creamy ricotta and mascarpone and you've got a pizza that beats a biscuit any day, any time.

½   cup ricotta cheese

¼   cup mascarpone

1   tablespoon honey

¼   cup uncooked grits or polenta, for rolling the dough

1   ball prepared pizza dough, at room temperature

2   tablespoons olive oil

½   cup fig jam

8   fresh figs, cut in half, or 6 dried figs, sliced on an angle as thinly as possible (try to get 4 slices per fig)

6   ounces country ham, thinly sliced (about 5 biscuit-size slices) and broken into pieces or diced

¼   cup walnut halves, toasted (page 181) and roughly chopped

    Kosher salt and freshly ground black pepper to taste

ADVENTURE CLUB Saute the figs in butter with a sprinkling of sugar or poach in red wine (page 181).

DRINK THIS This uncommon pizza balances sweet, savory, and salty flavors—and pairs perfectly with the slightly effervescent Moscato d'Asti from Italy.

In a medium bowl, combine the ricotta, mascarpone, and honey until smooth. Reserve for topping.

Preheat the grill, roll out and shape the dough, and grill the first side of the crust per the master instructions on page 11 for gas or page 14 for charcoal. Use tongs to transfer it to a peel or rimless baking sheet. Flip the crust to reveal the grilled side.

Spread the entire surface with the jam. Artfully arrange the fig slices on top and sprinkle with the ham and walnuts. Spoon small dollops of the ricotta-mascarpone mixture over the top.

Finish grilling the pizza per the master instructions.

Remove from the grill and season with pepper. Since the ham is salty, taste first, then salt only if necessary. Slice and serve immediately.

Note: If you don't have access to country ham in your part of the United States, substitute thick-sliced prosciutto or order it by mail (www.countryham.org).

Pulled Pork Pizza

Serves 2 to 4

We've combined the tangy vinegar sauce of Carolina pulled pork and the tomato-based flavor of Memphis BBQ. Try this pizza with leftover pulled pork, or shake up your next backyard BBQ and serve pulled pork pizza instead of the traditional sandwich.

2   cups (leftover) North Carolina–Style Pulled Pork (page 170) or store-bought

¼   cup Carolina Vinegar Sauce (page 171)

¼   cup uncooked grits or polenta, for rolling the dough

1   ball prepared pizza dough, at room temperature

2   tablespoons olive oil

½   cup tomato-based BBQ sauce (use your favorite store-bought or homemade)

4   scallions (white and green parts), thinly sliced

1½ cups grated Fontina cheese

1   cup Carolina Coleslaw (page 171)

Kosher salt and freshly ground black pepper to taste

Mix the pulled pork with the vinegar sauce. Reserve for topping.

Preheat the grill, roll out and shape the dough, and grill the first side of the crust per the master instructions on page 11 for gas or page 14 for charcoal. Use tongs to transfer it to a peel or rimless baking sheet. Flip the crust to reveal the grilled side.

Spread the entire surface with the BBQ sauce. Add the pork and scallions, and sprinkle with the cheese.

Finish grilling the pizza per the master instructions.

Remove from the grill. Strew the coleslaw about evenly and season with salt and pepper. Slice and serve immediately.

ADVENTURE CLUB Use Berkshire (heirloom) pork to make the pulled pork.

DRINK THIS "Lynchburg Lemonade"—a blend of lemonade and Jack Daniel's®—is what every self-respecting Southerner would serve with this pizza. Actually, true self-respecting Southerners drink their Jack straight, but we don't want to be a bad influence.

TASTES LIKE CHICKEN

Chicken is the little black dress of pizza.
It goes everywhere, and with everything.

Chicken Caesar Pizza

Serves 2 to 4 ✕

The pungent tanginess of a well-made Caesar salad is a restaurant staple. In this pizza, the grilled crust stands in for the croutons and the Parmigiano-Reggiano melts into the chicken for a more intense Caesar experience, one that Brutus would never betray.

1   large boneless, skinless chicken breast (about 12 ounces) or 1½ cups shredded leftover Beer Can Chicken (page 168) or any sliced cooked chicken breast

3   tablespoons olive oil, divided

Kosher salt and freshly ground black pepper to taste

¼   cup uncooked grits or polenta, for rolling the dough

1   ball prepared pizza dough, at room temperature

½   cup Roasted Garlic Paste (page 164)

1¼ cups grated Fontina cheese

1   heart of romaine, cut crosswise into ½-inch-wide ribbons

2   tablespoons Caesar Salad Dressing (page 169) or store-bought

2   tablespoons freshly grated Parmigiano-Reggiano cheese

ADVENTURE CLUB Top the salad greens with anchovies (and if you are really, really adventurous, use white anchovies).

DRINK THIS A not-too-oaky California Chardonnay, like many of our favorites from Santa Barbara, will make this Caesar salivate.

If you're not using leftover chicken, preheat the grill per the master instructions for gas (page 11) or charcoal (page 14).

Brush the chicken breast with 1 tablespoon of the oil and season with salt and pepper. Place the chicken on the cooking grate directly over the heat and grill until no longer pink in the middle, 10 to 12 minutes. Set aside and, when almost ready to use, cut into ¼-inch-thick strips.

Roll out and shape the dough, then grill the first side of the crust per the master instructions. Use tongs to transfer it from the grill to a peel or rimless baking sheet. Flip the crust to reveal the grilled side.

Spread the entire surface with the garlic paste, then top with the chicken and sprinkle with the Fontina.

Finish grilling the pizza per the master instructions.

Just before the pizza is done, toss the romaine with the dressing and 1 tablespoon of the Parmigiano in a medium bowl.

Remove the pizza from the grill and immediately top with dressed romaine. Sprinkle with the remaining 1 tablespoon Parmigiano and season with salt and pepper. Slice and serve immediately.

Kansas City BBQ Chicken Pizza

Serves 2 to 4 😊

Kansas City is best known for its sweet tomato BBQ sauce and for smokin' anything that moves. This BBQ pizza is slathered with a rich KC-style sauce and topped with chicken. We would have topped it with brisket but we weren't fast enough (to catch it)!

1   large boneless, skinless chicken breast (about 12 ounces) or 1½ cups shredded leftover Beer Can Chicken (page 168) or any sliced cooked chicken breast

3   tablespoons olive oil, divided

     Kosher salt and freshly ground black pepper to taste

¼   cup uncooked grits or polenta, for rolling the dough

1   ball prepared pizza dough, at room temperature

½   cup BBQ sauce (try Virginia Gentleman® Original BBQ Sauce)

1   cup grated smoked mozzarella

1   cup grated colby Jack cheese

⅓   medium red onion, cut ⅛ inch thick and separated into rings

½   bell pepper (any color), halved, seeded, and cut into very thin strips

     BBQ rub or red pepper flakes

ADVENTURE CLUB Replace the chicken breast with smoked chicken thighs.

DRINK THIS Zinfandel is known as "the BBQ grape." Who are we to argue?

If you're not using leftover chicken, preheat the grill per the master instructions for gas (page 11) or charcoal (page 14).

Brush the chicken breast with 1 tablespoon of the oil and season with salt and pepper.

Place the chicken on the cooking grate directly over the heat and grill until no longer pink in the middle, 10 to 12 minutes, turning once halfway through. Set aside until just about ready to use, then cut into ¼-inch-thick strips.

Roll out and shape the dough, then grill the first side of the crust per the master instructions. Use tongs to transfer it from the grill to a peel or rimless baking sheet. Flip the crust to reveal the grilled side.

Brush the entire surface with the BBQ sauce. Top with the chicken and sprinkle with the cheeses. Arrange the onion rings and all of the bell pepper over the cheese.

Finish grilling the pizza per the master instructions.

Remove from the grill, sprinkle with the BBQ rub, and season with salt and pepper. Slice and serve immediately.

Thai One On Pizza

Serves 2 to 4

We love Thai food so much that we couldn't resist taking the predominant flavors from our favorite dishes and giving them an American-style makeover.

½ cup peanut butter (ideally natural)

1 tablespoon Thai chili garlic sauce (Sriracha)

6 tablespoons canned unsweetened coconut milk

¼ teaspoon kosher salt, plus more to taste

¼ cup uncooked grits or polenta, for rolling the dough

1 ball prepared pizza dough, at room temperature

2 tablespoons olive oil

1½ cups sliced or shredded cooked chicken

1 ripe mango, peeled, pitted, and cut into matchstick-size slices

3 scallions (white and green parts), sliced thinly on an angle

1 cup grated mozzarella cheese

½ cup fresh bean sprouts

12 fresh mint leaves, cut into ribbons

2 tablespoons dry-roasted peanuts, chopped

1 lime, cut into 4 wedges

In a medium bowl, combine the peanut butter, chili garlic sauce, coconut milk, and salt. Reserve for topping.

Preheat the grill, roll out and shape the dough, and grill the first side of the crust per the master instructions on page 11 for gas or page 14 for charcoal. Use tongs to transfer it to a peel or rimless baking sheet. Flip the crust to reveal the grilled side.

Spread the entire surface with the peanut sauce. Top with the chicken, mango, and scallions. Sprinkle with the cheese.

Finish grilling the pizza per the master instructions.

Remove from the grill, sprinkle with the bean sprouts, mint, and nuts, and season with salt. Slice and serve immediately with the lime wedges for some extra zing.

ADVENTURE CLUB Top with some insanely hot Thai bird chiles, thinly sliced.

DRINK THIS We can't think of Thai cuisine without thinking about Thai beer. Singha® and Chang® are two of the best, and are generally available in North America.

Dixie Chicken Pizza

Serves 2 to 4 ⭐

This Southern belle certainly knows how to live high on the hog! She features a bourbon-spiked sweet potato base, crispy popcorn chicken, and our favorite new pizza topping: crumbled pork rinds. Lord have mercy!

1   cup Sweet Potato Bourbon Mash (page 172)

½   cup mascarpone

¼   cup uncooked grits or polenta, for rolling the dough

1   ball prepared pizza dough, at room temperature

3   tablespoons olive oil

1½   cups Popcorn Chicken (page 173) or purchased from your favorite chicken shack

1½   cups grated sharp white Cheddar cheese

½   cup crumbled pork rinds (pork rinds are available in the snack foods aisle of most grocery stores)

¼   cup maple syrup

      Freshly ground black pepper

ADVENTURE CLUB Sprinkle with chopped Sugar & Spice Pecans (page 139).

DRINK THIS You don't have to live in Tennessee to enjoy Lynchburg Lemonade. Make your own with your favorite bourbon and homemade lemonade.

In a medium-size bowl, mix the sweet potato mash and mascarpone. Reserve.

Preheat the grill per the master instructions for gas (page 11) or charcoal (page 14). Roll out and shape the dough, then grill the first side of the crust per the master instructions. When the bottom is marked and browned, use tongs to transfer the crust to a peel or rimless baking sheet. Switch the grill to indirect heat and close the lid to maintain the grill temperature.

Flip the crust to reveal the grilled side. Spread the entire surface with the sweet potato mixture. Top with popcorn chicken and sprinkle cheese over top.

Finish grilling the pizza per the master instructions.

Remove the pizza from the grill, sprinkle with the crumbled pork rinds, drizzle with maple syrup, and season with freshly ground pepper. Slice and serve immediately.

Note: Store-bought chicken and packaged pork rinds may contain gluten. If you are gluten-intolerant, make from scratch with your favorite gluten-free products.

Oy Vay! Pizza

Serves 2 to 4

This one is SO chopped liver. As with our Smokin' Salmon Pizza (page 64), only the crust is grilled, then the pizza is schmeared with chopped liver and quickly assembled. It's a mitzvah for any party host.

2	tablespoons melted butter
1	tablespoon brandy or cognac
¼	cup uncooked grits or polenta, for rolling the dough
1	ball prepared pizza dough, at room temperature
2	tablespoons olive oil
1	cup chicken liver pâté (page 172) or store-bought
4	hard-boiled eggs, sliced with an egg slicer
12	cornichons, sliced in half lengthwise
3	chives, finely diced
	Kosher salt

ADVENTURE CLUB Replace the chicken liver paté with paté de fois gras.

DRINK THIS Manischewitz isn't just for Passover any more!

Mix the melted butter and brandy and set aside on the pilot light of a gas range or a low burner to keep the brandy butter warm.

Preheat the grill per the master instructions for gas (page 11) or charcoal (page 14). Roll out and shape the dough, then grill the first side of the crust per the master instructions. When the bottom is marked and browned, flip the crust and grill until the second side is well browned, 2 to 3 minutes. (Since you're not melting cheese or warming any toppings, you don't need to switch to indirect heat for a gas grill.)

Remove the crust from the grill and immediately spread the entire surface with the pâté. Artfully arrange the egg slices and cornichons over top. Drizzle with the brandy butter and finish with chives and salt. Slice and serve immediately.

Kung Pao Cashew Chicken Pizza

Serves 2 to 4

What happens when you combine America's two favorite take-out foods? You end up with a fresh, crunchy, sweet, and spicy pizza that definitely won't leave you hungry in an hour.

¼ cup uncooked grits or polenta, for rolling the dough

1 ball prepared pizza dough, at room temperature

2 tablespoons olive oil

½ cup hoisin sauce (try Chinese markets for not-so-sweet versions)

1 teaspoon red pepper flakes

1 cup cubed cooked chicken (leftover from a roasted or rotisserie chicken)

3 scallions (white and green parts), thinly sliced on an angle

¼ red bell pepper, seeded and cut into paper-thin strips

½ cup grated mozzarella cheese

¼ cup fresh cilantro leaves

½ cup Thai Hot Chile–Lime Cashews (page 140) or unsalted dry-roasted cashews

   Kosher salt and freshly ground pepper (Sichuan if available) to taste

1 tablespoon toasted sesame oil

Preheat the grill, roll out and shape the dough, and grill the first side of the crust per the master instructions on page 11 for gas or page 14 for charcoal. Use tongs to transfer it to a peel or rimless baking sheet. Flip the crust to reveal the grilled side.

Spread the entire surface with the hoisin and sprinkle with the red pepper. Top with the chicken, scallions, and pepper strips. Sprinkle with the cheese.

Finish grilling the pizza per the master instructions.

Remove from the grill, sprinkle with the cilantro and cashews, and season with salt and black pepper. Drizzle with the sesame oil, slice, and serve immediately.

ADVENTURE CLUB Turn this into Kung Pao Shrimp Pizza by replacing the chicken with grilled shrimp.

DRINK THIS Confucius says, pair this pizza with a Chinese beer such as Tsingtao®.

Bollywood Chutney Chicken Pizza

Serves 2 to 4

Indian flavors and Bollywood movies are popular in America—and for good reason. Both are richly layered, colorful, spicy, and slightly chaotic. Why not take a break from the ordinary by making this pizza and watching a Bollywood classic?

¾ cup plain full-fat yogurt

1 teaspoon garam masala (an Indian spice blend)

1 teaspoon cracked coriander seeds

1 medium white onion, thinly sliced

2 tablespoons peeled and grated fresh ginger

2 cloves garlic, minced

   Juice of 1 lemon

2 teaspoons kosher salt

1 teaspoon turmeric

2 boneless, skinless chicken breast halves (1 pound total)

¼ cup uncooked grits or polenta, for rolling the dough

1 ball prepared pizza dough, at room temperature

2 tablespoons olive oil

1 cup mango chutney (Major Grey's®)

½ cup grated smoked mozzarella cheese

1 ripe mango, peeled, pitted, and diced

   Leaves from 3 sprigs fresh mint

¼ teaspoon red pepper flakes

In a large bowl, combine the yogurt, garam masala, coriander, half the onion, the ginger, garlic, lemon juice, salt, and turmeric. Add the chicken and stir to coat. Cover and refrigerate for 2 hours.

Thirty minutes before you want to make the pizza, preheat the grill per the master instructions for gas (page 11) or charcoal (page 14).

Remove the chicken from the marinade and place on the cooking grate directly over the heat. Grill until no pink remains in the middle, 5 to 8 minutes per side, depending on thickness. Reserve for topping and slice just before topping.

Roll out and shape the dough, then grill the first side of the crust per the master instructions. Use tongs to transfer it from the grill to a peel or rimless baking sheet. Flip the crust to reveal the grilled side.

Spread the entire surface with the chutney. Top with the chicken and the remaining onion. Sprinkle with the cheese and diced mango.

Finish grilling the pizza per the master instructions.

Remove from the grill and sprinkle with the mint and red pepper. Slice and serve immediately.

ADVENTURE CLUB Knead ¼ cup caramelized onions into the dough.

DRINK THIS Spicy Indian food is traditionally paired with a mango lassi—a delicious sweet and fruity yogurt smoothie—or sweeter white wines to temper the heat. Our favorite wine for this is a Kabinett-style German Riesling.

Day-after-Thanksgiving Pizza

Serves 2 to 4 ✕

All your favorite Thanksgiving leftovers together on a grilled pizza crust. Gobble, gobble!

½ cup Autumn Cranberry Chutney (page 177) or leftover cranberry sauce

1 cup Onion Marmalade (page 166)

¼ cup uncooked grits or polenta, for rolling the dough

1 ball prepared pizza dough, at room temperature

3 tablespoons olive oil

2 cups shredded leftover turkey

½ cup Southern Sausage Dressing (page 178) or leftover dressing or stuffing

6 ounces grated Comté cheese, or whatever cheese you have left over

1 celery rib, thinly sliced

¼ cup Pan Gravy (page 179) or leftover gravy

Kosher salt and freshly black ground pepper

ADVENTURE CLUB Top with slivers of pumpkin pie.

DRINK THIS Any leftover wine from your Thanksgiving dinner.

Mix the chutney and the marmalade. Reserve.

Preheat the grill per the master instructions for gas (page 11) or charcoal (page 14). Roll out and shape the dough, then grill the first side of the crust per the master instructions. When the bottom is marked and browned, use tongs to transfer the crust to a peel or rimless baking sheet.

Switch the grill to indirect heat and close the lid to maintain the grill temperature.

Flip the crust to reveal the grilled side. Spread the entire surface with the chutney-marmalade mixture. Top with the turkey, then crumble the dressing over top and sprinkle with the cheese and celery.

Finish grilling the pizza per the master instructions.

In a small pot or a microwave, warm the gravy.

Remove the pizza from the grill and drizzle with the gravy. Season with salt and pepper. Slice and serve immediately.

Note: Premade stuffing, as well as many other Thanksgiving foods, may contain gluten. If you are gluten-intolerant, make from scratch with your favorite gluten-free products.

Ring of Fire Pizza

Serves 2 to 4 ⭐

This ultimate heat-seeker's pizza combines the addictiveness of hot wings and the endorphin rush of a chile-pepper eating contest. It's guaranteed to ignite you on the way in—and the way out!

2	cups Frank's Red Hot® sauce
4	boneless skinless chicken thighs, about 12 ounces
3	poblano peppers
½	cup Roasted Garlic Paste (page 164)
¼	cup uncooked grits or polenta, for rolling the dough
1	ball prepared pizza dough, at room temperature
3	tablespoons olive oil
2	red jalapeños, sliced crosswise into thin rings (discard the seeds for less heat)
1-2	serrano peppers, sliced crosswise into thin rings (discard the seeds for less heat)
2	banana peppers, sliced crosswise into thin rings (discard the seeds for less heat)
1½	cups grated jalapeño Jack cheese
¼	cup Hot Pepper Jelly Glaze (page 176)
	Kosher salt

ADVENTURE CLUB Add some habanera or Thai bird's eye chiles to the mix.

DRINK THIS Beer…lots of it!

In a small pot, bring the hot sauce to a boil, add the chicken thighs, and then reduce the heat and simmer for 10 minutes, or until the chicken is cooked throughout. Let cool in the liquid, then remove and pull the thighs apart into bite-size pieces. Reserve.

Roast the poblanos as instructed on page 167, then peel and seed. Add to a food processor and puree along with the roasted garlic base. Reserve.

Preheat the grill per the master instructions for gas (page 11) or charcoal (page 14).

Roll out and shape the dough, then grill the first side of the crust per the master instructions. When the bottom is marked and browned, use tongs to transfer the crust to a peel or rimless baking sheet. Switch the grill to indirect heat and close the lid to maintain the grill temperature.

Flip the crust to reveal the grilled side. Spread the entire surface with the roasted garlic/poblano paste. Top with the chicken and the jalapeños, serranos, and banana peppers. Sprinkle with the cheese and return to the grill.

Finish grilling the pizza per the master instructions.

Remove from the grill, drizzle with the hot pepper jelly glaze, and season lightly with salt. Slice and serve immediately.

Duck Duck Pizza

Serves 2 to 4

This one isn't child's play. It's everything you love about duck confit, swaddled in a grown-up cassis sauce.

¼ cup uncooked grits or polenta, for rolling the dough

1 ball prepared pizza dough, at room temperature

3 tablespoons olive oil

¾ cup Cassis Sauce (page 177)

1½ cups shredded duck confit or roasted duck

½ cup sliced water chestnuts, cut into slivers

8 ounces St. André cheese (a French triple-crème), rind removed if preferred, cut into ¼-inch-thick strips, then cut into 1-inch squares

3 scallions, trimmed, cleaned, and sliced

Zest of 1 mandarin orange or clementine

Kosher salt and freshly ground black pepper

DRINK THIS The red wines from France's under-rated Languedoc region are rich and powerful, and deliver great bang for your duck.

Preheat the grill per the master instructions for gas (page 11) or charcoal (page 14). Roll out and shape the dough, then grill the first side of the crust per the master instructions. When the bottom is marked and browned, use tongs to transfer the crust to a peel or rimless baking sheet. Switch the grill to indirect heat and close the lid to maintain the grill temperature.

Flip the crust to reveal the grilled side. Spread the entire surface with cassis sauce. Top with the duck, sprinkle with water chestnuts, and top with cheese.

Finish grilling the pizza per the master instructions. Remove from the grill.

Sprinkle the scallions and zest evenly over the pizza. Season with salt and pepper. Slice and serve immediately.

ADVENTURE CLUB Make your own duck confit.

BIG & BEEFY PIZZAS

These meaty pizzas will satisfy both your steakhouse and burger shack cravings.

Black 'n' Blue Steak Pizza

Serves 2 to 4 ⭐

Grilled steak and blue cheese are steakhouse staples. They conjure up thoughts of birthdays, anniversaries, and big expense-account dinners. This pizza will feed four discriminating diners with one prime steak, making it a luxury you can afford any night of the week.

1   16-ounce prime sirloin steak, 1½ inches thick

3   tablespoons olive oil, divided

     Kosher salt to taste

¼   cup uncooked grits or polenta, for rolling the dough

1   ball prepared pizza dough, at room temperature

½   cup Roasted Garlic Paste (page 164)

½   cup Onion Marmalade (page 166)

1   cup crumbled Roquefort cheese (about 4 ounces)

2   tablespoons finely chopped fresh parsley

     Freshly ground black pepper to taste

ADVENTURE CLUB Replace the sirloin with prime rib and the Roquefort with horseradish cream.

DRINK THIS Get the biggest, baddest California Cab you can afford with all the money you've saved by eating in.

At least 30 minutes before making the pizza, bring the steak to room temperature.

Preheat the grill per the master instructions for gas (page 11) or charcoal (page 14).

Brush the steak lightly with 1 tablespoon of the oil and season with salt. Place it on the cooking grate directly over the heat and grill for about 6 minutes per side. Because the steak will cook again on the pizza, remove it from the grill when it is slightly less cooked than your desired degree of doneness. Let rest, loosely covered with aluminum foil, for 30 minutes. Just before making the pizza, cut into ¼-inch-thick slices.

Roll out and shape the dough, then grill the first side of the crust per the master instructions. Use tongs to transfer it from the grill to a peel or rimless baking sheet. Flip the crust to reveal the grilled side.

Spread the entire surface with the garlic paste, then with the marmalade. Artfully arrange the steak slices over the top and sprinkle with the cheese.

Finish grilling the pizza per the master instructions.

Remove from the grill, sprinkle with the parsley, and season with salt and pepper. Slice and serve immediately.

Bacon Cheeseburger in Paradizza

Serves 2 to 4 😊 ✕

This is a pizza any parrot-head will love.

2   ½-inch-thick slices red onion, separated into rings

3   tablespoons olive oil, divided

     Kosher salt to taste; more as needed

1   pound ground chuck (or other ground beef)

1   tablespoon Worcestershire sauce

1½   teaspoons Colman's® dry mustard

½   teaspoon onion powder

     Pinch of freshly ground black pepper; more to taste

¼   cup uncooked grits or polenta, for rolling the dough

1   ball prepared pizza dough, at room temperature

¾   cup Tuscan Red Sauce (page 159) or Crushed Tomato Sauce (page 160)

4   3-inch-square packaged Cheddar cheese slices

8   strips center-cut bacon, cooked until crisp

1   dill pickle, sliced crosswise

ADVENTURE CLUB Replace the ground chuck with ground aged prime beef.

DRINK THIS Nothing is more kid friendly— or pleasing to big kids—than a chocolate milkshake.

Preheat the grill per the master instructions for gas (page 11) or charcoal (page 14).

Lightly brush the onion rings with 1 tablespoon of the oil and season with salt. Place on the cooking grate directly over the heat and grill until browned and slightly caramelized, 2 to 3 minutes per side. Reserve for topping.

Mix together the ground meat, Worcestershire, mustard, onion powder, ½ teaspoon salt, and a pinch of pepper until well combined. Preheat a large sauté pan over medium-high heat. Add the hamburger mixture and cook, stirring occasionally and breaking up any clumps of meat, until no longer pink. Let cool and reserve for topping.

Roll out and shape the dough, then grill the first side of the crust per the master instructions. Use tongs to transfer it from the grill to a peel or rimless baking sheet. Flip the crust to reveal the grilled side.

Spread the entire surface with the sauce. Top with the hamburger mixture. Place the squares of cheese in a square-like pattern, making sure not to overlap them. Top each with 2 strips of bacon and a grilled onion ring so the pizza resembles 4 bacon cheeseburgers.

Finish grilling the pizza per the master instructions.

Remove from the grill, garnish with the pickle slices, and season with salt and pepper. Slice and serve immediately.

Nacho Libre Pizza

Serves 2 to 4

If you like nachos piled up on a plate, you will love a slice of this deluxe version on a pizza.

¼ cup uncooked grits or polenta, for rolling the dough

1 ball prepared pizza dough, at room temperature

2 tablespoons olive oil

1 cup refried beans, homemade or store-bought

1 cup salsa, homemade or store-bought

1½ cups cooked ground beef or shredded leftover chicken

1 tablespoon chili powder

1½ cups grated jalapeño Jack cheese

½ cup sliced black olives, drained

½ cup frozen corn kernels, thawed

Pickled jalapeño slices (about 20)

2 tablespoons chopped fresh cilantro

Preheat the grill, roll out and shape the dough, and grill the first side of the crust per the master instructions on page 11 for gas or page 14 for charcoal. Use tongs to transfer it to a peel or rimless baking sheet. Flip the crust to reveal the grilled side.

Spread the entire surface with the refried beans. Top with the salsa, meat, chili powder, cheese, olives, and corn.

Finish grilling the pizza per the master instructions.

Remove from the grill. Sprinkle with the jalapeños and cilantro. Slice and serve immediately.

ADVENTURE CLUB Mix ½ cup sour cream with 2 teaspoons fresh lime juice. Transfer to a squirt bottle and use it to sign your name on the finished pizza.

DRINK THIS Try as we may, we can't think of anything better than the King of Beers for this "king of bar snacks" pizza.

Gaucho Pizza

Serves 2 to 4 ☆

Gauchos are Argentinean cowboys who herd cattle across the plains to the seaports. Along the way they feed themselves with spit-grilled beef. We tip our cowboy hats to these rugged gauchos by taking it one step further and dressing up grilled flank steak with the fresh herbal taste of chimichurri sauce—the national condiment of Argentina.

1	teaspoon cumin seeds
1	teaspoon granulated garlic
2	teaspoons smoked paprika (pimentón); more to taste
¼	cup olive oil, divided
1	1-pound flank steak
¼	cup uncooked grits or polenta, for rolling the dough
1	ball prepared pizza dough, at room temperature
¾	cup Chimichurri Sauce (page 169)
½	cup Fontina cheese, grated
6	cherry tomatoes, sliced
	Kosher salt and freshly ground pepper to taste

ADVENTURE CLUB Use grass-fed beef, ideally from Argentina.

DRINK THIS An Argentinean Syrah with notes of leather and spice is a nice choice for this grill fest.

Preheat the grill per the master instructions for gas (page 11) or charcoal (page 14).

In a small bowl, combine the cumin seeds, granulated garlic, and paprika. Brush the meat lightly with 1 to 2 tablespoons of the oil, season with salt, then sprinkle generously with the spice mixture. Place the steak on the cooking grate directly over the heat and grill for about 6 minutes per side. Because the steak will cook again on the pizza, remove it from the grill when it is slightly less cooked than your desired degree of doneness. Let rest for 30 minutes. Just before making the pizza, cut into ¼-inch-thick slices.

Roll out and shape the dough, then grill the first side of the crust per the master instructions. Use tongs to transfer it from the grill to a peel or rimless baking sheet. Flip the crust to reveal the grilled side.

Spread the entire surface with the chimichurri. Artfully arrange the steak slices and tomatoes on top and sprinkle with the cheese.

Finish grilling the pizza per the master instructions.

Remove from the grill, finish with a dusting of paprika, and season with salt and pepper. Slice and serve immediately.

Mo'roccan Pizza

Serves 2 to 4 ⭐

Uncover the lid of any simmering tagine in Morocco and you are bound to be seduced by the heady aromas. Under the lid you'll discover some form of lamb accented with dried fruits and a blend of traditional spices. Here's lookin' at you—and your pizza—kid.

4	tablespoons olive oil, divided
1	small yellow onion, diced
½	teaspoon kosher salt
1	pound ground lamb
1	teaspoon ground cinnamon
¼	teaspoon ground nutmeg
¼	teaspoon ground clove
½	cup dried apricots, sliced
¼	cup golden raisins
¼	cup uncooked grits or polenta, for rolling the dough
1	ball prepared pizza dough, at room temperature
¾	cup Pistachio Pesto with Mint (page 175) + extra mint and pistachios to finish
6	ounces Robiola cheese, grated

ADVENTURE CLUB Use merguez sausage that has been removed from its casing in place of ground lamb.

DRINK THIS Make a refreshing mint soda by combining green crème de menthe (or mint syrup) with club soda, and serve over ice.

In a medium sauté pan over medium heat, add 1 tablespoon of oil, the onions, and the salt, and cook until the onions begin to brown, about 5 minutes. Add the lamb and stir to combine. When the lamb begins to brown, add the spices, apricots, and raisins. Cover, reduce the heat to medium low, and cook, stirring occasionally, for about 10 minutes, or until the lamb is fully cooked. Transfer to a plate lined with paper towels to absorb excess fat. Reserve.

Preheat the grill per the master instructions for gas (page 11) or charcoal (page 14). Roll out and shape the dough, then grill the first side of the crust per the master instructions. When the bottom is marked and browned, use tongs to transfer the crust to a peel or rimless baking sheet. Switch the grill to indirect heat and close the lid to maintain the grill temperature.

Flip the crust to reveal the grilled side. Spread the entire surface with the pistachio mint pesto. Spread the lamb mixture over top, then top with the cheese.

Finish grilling the pizza per the master instructions.

Remove from the grill, then sprinkle with a smattering of pistachios and some mint leaves. Slice and serve immediately.

The Great Greek Pizza

Serves 2 to 4

Greek flavors are big and fat. Start with the usual suspects, then add ribbons of grilled zucchini to brighten and lighten the flavor. Every bite will transport you to the Greek islands.

12 ounces raw spicy lamb sausage (ideally merguez sausage)

1 small zucchini, cut lengthwise into thin ribbons with a vegetable peeler or mandoline

3 tablespoons olive oil, divided

Kosher salt to taste

¼ cup uncooked grits or polenta, for rolling the dough

1 ball prepared pizza dough, at room temperature

¼ cup Black Olive Purée (page 163) or store-bought tapenade

1½ cups grated smoked mozzarella cheese

½ small red onion, thinly sliced and separated into rings

12 cherry tomatoes, quartered, or ½ cup Tomato-Basil Base (page 159)

½ cup crumbled feta cheese

Leaves from 4 sprigs fresh oregano or 2 teaspoons dried

Freshly ground black pepper to taste

ADVENTURE CLUB Top with zucchini flowers.

DRINK THIS We can't resist serving Retsina, Greece's distinctive pine-scented wine. But be forewarned—it is definitely an acquired taste.

Preheat a medium sauté pan over medium-high heat for 1 to 2 minutes. Remove the sausage from the casing and "scramble" in the pan, breaking up any clumps, until fully cooked. Drain on paper towels and reserve for topping.

Preheat the grill per the master instructions for gas (page 11) or charcoal (page 14).

Brush the zucchini with 1 tablespoon of the oil and lightly salt. Gently place on the cooking grate directly over the heat and grill until soft and well marked, about 3 minutes. Reserve for topping.

Roll out and shape the dough, then grill the first side of the crust per the master instructions. Use tongs to transfer it from the grill to a peel or rimless baking sheet. Flip the crust to reveal the grilled side.

Spread the entire surface with the olive purée, then top with the crumbled lamb. Sprinkle with the mozzarella, then add the onion rings, zucchini, and tomatoes. Sprinkle the feta over all.

Finish grilling the pizza per the master instructions.

Remove from the grill, sprinkle with the oregano, and season with salt and pepper. Slice and serve immediately.

Marsala Meatball Pizza

Serves 2 to 4

Meatballs are SO in! This pizza takes the flavors of the old-school veal Marsala dish and turns it into a modern classic.

2   tablespoons unsalted butter

1½ cups sliced button mushrooms

    Kosher salt and freshly ground black pepper

¼   cup uncooked grits or polenta, for rolling the dough

1   ball prepared pizza dough, at room temperature

3   tablespoons olive oil

1   cup Fire-Roasted Vodka Sauce (page 176) or store-bought vodka sauce

15 Marsala Meatballs (page 174) or from your family meatball recipe, sliced in half

12 yellow cherry tomatoes, sliced in half

4   ounces Taleggio cheese, grated

½   cup freshly grated pecorino cheese

2   tablespoons chopped fresh parsley

ADVENTURE CLUB Replace the button mushrooms with porcini mushrooms.

DRINK THIS Marsala, Sicily's fortified wine, is commonly used in popular Italian dishes. But we also love to sip it.

In a sauté pan over medium-high heat, melt the butter, add the mushrooms, and season with salt and pepper. Cook, stirring occasionally, until browned on the edges, about 10 minutes. Reserve.

Preheat the grill per the master instructions for gas (page 11) or charcoal (page 14). Roll out and shape the dough, then grill the first side of the crust per the master instructions. When bottom is marked and browned, use tongs to transfer the crust to a peel or rimless baking sheet. Switch the grill to indirect heat and close the lid to maintain the grill temperature.

Flip the crust to reveal the grilled side. Spread the entire surface with the vodka sauce. Arrange the mushrooms over top of the sauce, then artfully arrange the meatball and tomato halves. Sprinkle with Taleggio.

Finish grilling the pizza per the master instructions. Remove from the grill. Finish with grated pecorino cheese and chopped parsley. Season with salt and pepper. Slice and serve immediately.

MORNING GLORIES

Breakfast pizzas have come a long way
from the cold leftover-pie-in-the-fridge days.

Artichoke Benedict Pizza

Serves 2 to 4 ⭐ 🍴

Nothing says Sunday brunch like eggs benedict. We like it so much that we hate waiting for the weekend. Fortunately for us, the richness of the artichoke spread makes this pizza suitable for breakfast, lunch, or dinner any day of the week.

4	cups water
1	tablespoon white vinegar or lemon juice
4	eggs
¼	cup uncooked grits or polenta, for rolling the dough
1	ball prepared pizza dough, at room temperature
2	tablespoons olive oil
1	cup Artichoke Spread (page 163) or store-bought (may be called "artichoke pesto")
1	cup fresh baby spinach, washed well and spun dry
1	cup grated white Cheddar cheese
2	tablespoons diced red Fire-Roasted Peppers (page 167) or store-bought
	Kosher salt and freshly ground black pepper to taste

ADVENTURE CLUB Top the pizza with strips of smoked salmon just before serving.

DRINK THIS Nothing accompanies a Benedict pizza like a Bloody Mary.

Bring the water and vinegar to a boil in a medium saucepan, reduce the heat to a simmer, gently slide the eggs into the simmering water one at a time, and poach until softly cooked, 2 to 3 minutes. Carefully remove from the water with a slotted spoon and reserve in a shallow bowl.

Preheat the grill, roll out and shape the dough, and grill the first side of the crust per the master instructions on page 11 for gas or page 14 for charcoal. Use tongs to transfer it to a peel or rimless baking sheet. Flip the crust to reveal the grilled side.

Spread the entire surface with the artichoke spread and the spinach. Sprinkle with the cheese.

Finish grilling the pizza per the master instructions for 8 minutes. Open the lid and slide the poached eggs onto the crust. Put the lid down and continue grilling until the bottom crust is well browned and the cheese melted, about 2 more minutes.

Remove from the grill, sprinkle with the roasted peppers, and season with salt and black pepper. Slice and serve immediately.

Cinn-O-Bun Pizza

Serves 2 to 4 🙂

Everything you love about warm-from-the-oven cinnamon rolls is on this pizza. Sure it takes a bit of time to prepare the ingredients from scratch, but that's what makes it *cinnfully* delicious.

¼ cup apple cider or juice

½ cup water

¾ cup raisins or dried cherries

3 tablespoons granulated sugar

2 teaspoons ground cinnamon

¼ cup (½ stick) unsalted butter, softened

¾ cup confectioners' sugar

 Pinch of sea salt

3 tablespoons heavy cream

½ teaspoon vanilla extract

¼ cup all-purpose flour, for rolling the dough

1 ball prepared pizza dough, at room temperature

2 tablespoons walnut oil

¾ cup pecan pieces, toasted (page 181)

⅓ cup Caramel Sauce (page 165) or store-bought

ADVENTURE CLUB Poach your raisins in rum instead of apple cider.

DRINK THIS Whether you are enjoying this sweet pizza for breakfast or dessert, it fares best with a strong cup of joe.

Combine the cider and water in a small saucepan. Add the raisins, bring to a low boil, reduce the heat to low, cover, and let simmer until the fruit is plump and has absorbed the cider mixture, about 20 minutes. Drain and reserve for topping.

Combine the sugar and cinnamon in a small bowl. Add the butter and mix with a fork until completely smooth. Reserve for topping.

Mix the confectioners' sugar, a pinch of salt, the cream, and vanilla together in a medium bowl until smooth. If too thick to drizzle, add a little more cream; if too loose, add a little more sugar until you have the right consistency. Reserve for topping.

Preheat the grill, roll out and shape the dough, and brush on 1 tablespoon walnut oil. Grill the first side of the crust per the master instructions on page 11 for gas or page 14 for charcoal. Use tongs to turn the crust over; brush the remaining walnut oil on the crust. Continue grilling until the bottom crust is lightly browned, 2 to 3 minutes. Use tongs to transfer the crust from the grill to a peel or rimless baking sheet.

Immediately spread the entire surface with the cinnamon-sugar butter mixture. Top with the raisins and scatter with the pecans. Drizzle all over with the caramel sauce. Finish grilling the pizza per the master instructions, cooking just until the toppings are warmed through, about 3 minutes.

Remove from the grill and generously drizzle with the icing. Slice and serve immediately. Yummmm.

Green Eggs & Ham Pizza

Serves 2 to 4 ☺

Scrambled eggs on a croissant is so last millennium. This breakfast pizza combines the best qualities of a fresh herb omelet, broiled tomatoes, and ham into one fabulously contemporary morning meal that would make any cat tip his hat to the cook.

6   eggs

     Kosher salt and freshly ground black pepper to taste

3   tablespoons olive oil, divided

3   tablespoons finely chopped fresh dill (or tarragon, chervil, or your favorite green herb)

3   tablespoons finely chopped fresh chives

3   tablespoons finely chopped fresh parsley

¼   cup uncooked grits or polenta, for rolling the dough

1   ball prepared pizza dough, at room temperature

½   cup Tuscan Red Sauce (page 159) or Crushed Tomato Sauce (page 160)

6   ounces goat or any Brie cheese, rind removed if preferred, cut into ¼-inch-thick strips, then cut into 1-inch pieces

2   ounces thinly sliced prosciutto or country ham

ADVENTURE CLUB Top with dollops of crème fraîche and salmon caviar just before serving.

DRINK THIS Do you like champagne and O.J.? They're quite the combo, dare we say.

Just before you make the pizza, beat the eggs together in a medium bowl and season with salt and pepper. Preheat a large sauté pan over medium-high heat, add 1 tablespoon of the oil, and swirl the pan to coat the bottom. Add the eggs and all the herbs. Stir and scramble until the eggs are no longer wet. Do not overcook. Remove from the heat, cover the pan, and reserve for topping.

Preheat the grill, roll out and shape the dough, and grill the first side of the crust per the master instructions on page 11 for gas or page 14 for charcoal. Use tongs to transfer it to a peel or rimless baking sheet. Flip the crust to reveal the grilled side.

Spread the entire surface with the sauce and top with the cheese.

Finish grilling the pizza per the master instructions.

Remove from the grill, spoon the still-warm eggs over the top, and place the prosciutto slices over the eggs. Season with salt and pepper. Slice and serve immediately.

SWEET THANGS
Pizza as a dessert.
Delicious any way you slice it.

Funky Monkey Pizza

Serves 2 to 4

We can't decide what satisfies our sweet tooth more—tropical rainforest crunch candy or Ben & Jerry's® Chunky Monkey® ice cream. Because we like to monkey around in the kitchen, we took the best of both and turned them into a dessert pizza that proves that sometimes more is more.

¼ cup all-purpose flour, for rolling the dough

¼ cup semisweet or bittersweet chocolate chips

1 ball prepared pizza dough, at room temperature

2 tablespoons vegetable oil (such as canola) or nut oil (such as walnut)

½ cup Chocolate Ganache (page 165) or store-bought chocolate sauce

½ cup crunchy peanut butter

¼ cup dry-roasted cashews

¼ cup walnut halves, toasted (page 181)

2 ripe bananas, peeled and cut into thin diagonal slices

½ cup coarsely grated white chocolate

¼ cup sweetened flaked coconut, toasted (page 181)

Fleur de sel or kosher salt to taste

Sprinkle the work surface with the flour. Knead the chocolate chips into the dough, then set aside until ready to make the pizza.

Preheat the grill, roll out and shape the dough, and grill the first side of the crust per the master instructions on page 11 for gas or page 14 for charcoal. Use tongs to turn the crust over. Continue grilling until the bottom crust is lightly browned, 2 to 3 minutes. Use tongs to transfer the crust from the grill to a peel or rimless baking sheet.

Spread the entire surface with the ganache, then the peanut butter. Sprinkle with the nuts and artfully arrange the banana slices on top. Sprinkle with the white chocolate.

Finish grilling the pizza per the master instructions until the toppings are warm, about 3 minutes.

Remove from the grill, garnish with the coconut, and season lightly with salt. Let sit for 5 minutes so the toppings can settle before slicing and serving.

ADVENTURE CLUB Top with rocky road ice cream and call your dentist in the morning.

DRINK THIS Some things are just made for a glass of ice cold milk. This is one of them.

Port-Drizzled Fig & Stilton Pizza

Serves 2 to 4 ⭐

If you are skeptical about the notion of eating pizza for dessert, we hope you'll try this harmonious combination of bitter orange, sweet fig, and unctuous Stilton. We think it is the ultimate cheese course. If you are not completely convinced, call 1-800-I'LL-HAVE-VANILLA for a full refund.

1	cup port
¼	cup uncooked grits or polenta, for rolling the dough
1	ball prepared pizza dough, at room temperature
2	tablespoons vegetable oil (such as canola) or nut oil (such as walnut)
½	cup best-quality orange marmalade (try Dundee)
8	dried figs, sliced on an angle as thinly as possible (try to get 4 slices per fig)
1	cup crumbled Stilton cheese (about 4 ounces)
	Freshly ground black pepper to taste

ADVENTURE CLUB Replace the dried figs with fresh figs.

DRINK THIS Port with Stilton is one of the all-time classic pairings.

In a small saucepan over medium heat, reduce the port by three-quarters, until it has the thickness of maple syrup, about 20 minutes. Reserve half for topping and refrigerate the rest in an airtight container to use as a topping for ice cream, a drizzle for cheese, or on top of fresh berries.

Preheat the grill, roll out and shape the dough, and grill the first side of the crust per the master instructions on page 11 for gas or page 14 for charcoal. Use tongs to transfer it to a peel or rimless baking sheet. Flip the crust to reveal the grilled side.

Spread the entire surface with the marmalade. Artfully arrange the fig slices on top and sprinkle with the cheese.

Finish grilling the pizza per the master instructions.

Remove from the grill. Drizzle with the port reduction and season with pepper. Slice and serve immediately.

Orange Chocolate Truffle Pizza

Serves 2 to 4

You don't have to be a chocolatier to duplicate the flavors of a fancy orange truffle. The secret is the balance between sweet and bittersweet chocolate, and the aromatic infusion of orange.

¼ cup all-purpose flour, for rolling the dough

1 ball prepared pizza dough, at room temperature

2 tablespoons vegetable oil (such as canola) or nut oil (such as walnut)

¾ cup Nutella (chocolate hazelnut spread)

1 tablespoon Grand Marnier or other orange liqueur

2 ounces bittersweet chocolate (around 70% cocoa), broken into small pieces

¼ cup chopped hazelnuts, toasted (page 181)

Zest of 1 orange, finely grated with a Microplane or zester

Fleur de sel or kosher salt to taste

ADVENTURE CLUB Replace the zest with candied orange rind.

DRINK THIS Keep the Grand Marnier flowing.

Preheat the grill, roll out and shape the dough, and grill the first side of the crust per the master instructions on page 11 for gas or page 14 for charcoal. Use tongs to turn the crust over. Continue grilling until the bottom crust is lightly browned, 2 to 3 minutes. Use tongs to transfer the crust from the grill to a peel or rimless baking sheet.

Spread the entire surface with the Nutella, drizzle with the Grand Marnier, and sprinkle with the chocolate and nuts.

Finish grilling the pizza per the master instructions until the bottom is well browned and the chocolate has melted, about 3 minutes.

Remove from the grill, sprinkle with the orange zest, and season with salt (it may seem counterintuitive, but a little salt will work well with the chocolate). Slice and serve immediately.

Caramelized Pear & Roasted Walnut Pizza

Serves 2 to 4 ⭐

How much do we love this dessert pizza?! It is hard to believe that a pizza with three toppings can taste this complex and delicious. But this is a perfect example of our philosophy that time invested in homemade toppings is time well spent. It's so good, you'll find plenty of uses for the Walnut Spread, like on crêpes or waffles or spreading it on bread and adding sliced bananas.

2	ripe pears, peeled
¼	cup firmly packed dark brown sugar
2	tablespoons unsalted butter
1	tablespoon granulated sugar
½	teaspoon ground cinnamon, divided
1	ball prepared pizza dough, at room temperature
¼	cup all-purpose flour, for rolling the dough
1	cup Walnut Spread (page 168)
6	ounces Cambozola or Saga blue cheese, cut into ¼-inch-thick strips

ADVENTURE CLUB Finish with a crumble of your favorite toffee or a Heath bar.

DRINK THIS A late-harvest dessert wine, such as Tokaji from Hungary, Sauterne from France, or ice wine from Canada or Germany, would be a luscious accompaniment for the Walnut Spread and caramelized pears.

Stand each pear upright and cut vertically into ¼-inch-thick slices. Use a small spoon or paring knife to remove the core from the pear slices. Spread the brown sugar evenly on a small plate and dredge both sides of the pears in it to coat. In a large sauté pan over medium heat, melt the butter. When it bubbles, gently add the pears and cook until nicely browned and soft, about 4 minutes per side. Remove from the heat and reserve for topping.

Mix the granulated sugar with ¼ teaspoon of the cinnamon and knead into the dough. Set aside until ready to make pizza.

Preheat the grill, roll out and shape the dough, and grill the first side of the crust per the master instructions on page 11 for gas or page 14 for charcoal. (Brush the dough with 2 tablespoons walnut oil in place of olive oil.) Use tongs to transfer it to a peel or rimless baking sheet. Flip the crust to reveal the grilled side.

Spread the entire surface with the walnut spread. Artfully arrange the pear slices on top and sprinkle with the cheese.

Finish grilling the pizza per the master instructions.

Remove from the grill and sprinkle with the remaining ¼ teaspoon cinnamon. Slice and serve immediately.

Caramel Apple Pie Pizza (à la Mode)

Serves 2 to 4 ✕

American pie meets American pizza in this tricked-up version of the mother of all desserts.

6   Granny Smith apples, peeled, cored, and cut into ½-inch-thick slices

    Juice of ½ lemon

3   tablespoons sugar

¾   teaspoon ground cinnamon

2   tablespoons unsalted butter

¼   cup all-purpose flour, for rolling the dough

1   ball prepared pizza dough, at room temperature

2   tablespoons vegetable oil (such as canola) or nut oil (such as walnut)

¾   cup Caramel Sauce (page 165) or store-bought

¾   cup sliced almonds, toasted (page 181)

    Fleur de sel or best available salt to taste

1   cup best-quality vanilla ice cream or whipped cream

ADVENTURE CLUB Replace the caramel sauce with dulce de leche.

DRINK THIS Calvados is a fiery apple brandy from Normandy, France. A small snort of it is all you need to temper the sweetness of the caramel.

Place the apple slices in a large nonreactive metal or glass bowl. Add the lemon juice and toss to coat so the slices don't brown. Mix the sugar with the cinnamon, sprinkle 2 tablespoons of the mixture over the apples, and toss to coat.

Melt the butter in a large, heavy skillet over medium heat. When it bubbles, add the apple slices and the liquid that has collected in the bowl. Stir so all the slices are coated with butter. Let cook, stirring occasionally, until soft and slightly caramelized on the edges, about 10 minutes. Remove from the heat and reserve for topping.

Preheat the grill, roll out and shape the dough, and grill the first side of the crust per the master instructions on page 11 for gas or page 14 for charcoal. Use tongs to turn the crust over. Continue grilling until the bottom crust is lightly browned, 2 to 3 minutes. Use tongs to transfer the crust from the grill to a peel or rimless baking sheet.

Sprinkle the entire surface with the remaining cinnamon sugar, then spread with ½ cup of the caramel sauce. Artfully arrange the apples on top and sprinkle with the almonds. Drizzle over the remaining ¼ cup caramel sauce.

Finish grilling the pizza per the master instructions until the toppings are warm, about 3 minutes.

Remove from the grill and garnish with a light sprinkle of fleur de sel. Let sit for 5 minutes to let the caramel firm up. Slice and serve immediately topped with a spoonful of ice cream or whipped cream.

Very Berry Pizza

Serves 2 to 4 ☺

Now you can enjoy all your favorite antioxidants and eat your pizza too.

1   cup ricotta cheese

½   teaspoon vanilla extract

5   tablespoons sugar

2   tablespoons finely chopped crystallized
      ginger

      Zest of ½ lemon, finely grated with a Micro-
      plane or zester

2   tablespoons all-purpose flour, for kneading
      the dough

¾   teaspoon ground cinnamon

1   ball prepared pizza dough, at room
      temperature

¼   cup uncooked grits or polenta, for rolling
      the dough

2   tablespoons vegetable oil (such as canola)
      or nut oil (such as walnut)

½   pint fresh blueberries, picked over

½   pint fresh raspberries, picked over

¼   cup honey

Combine the ricotta, vanilla, 2 tablespoons of the sugar, the ginger, and lemon zest in a medium bowl. Reserve for topping.

Sprinkle the work surface with the flour. Mix the remaining 3 tablespoons sugar with the cinnamon and knead it into the dough. Set aside until ready to make pizza.

Preheat the grill, roll out and shape the dough, and grill the first side of the crust per the master instructions on page 11 for gas or page 14 for charcoal. Use tongs to turn the crust over. Continue grilling until the bottom crust is well browned. (Since you're not melting cheese or warming toppings, you don't need to switch to indirect heat.)

Remove from the grill and immediately spread it evenly with the ricotta mixture. Let your inner artist dictate how you arrange the berries over the top. Finish with a generous drizzle of honey. Slice and serve immediately.

ADVENTURE CLUB Add the pulp from 2 fresh passion fruits to the ricotta cheese mixture.

DRINK THIS Buy a few extra raspberries and make your own raspberry lemonade.

Sweetheart Pizza

Serves 2 to 4

Celebrate your love of pizza on Valentine's Day and all year long with this swoon-worthy, salted caramel and dark chocolate confection. S.W.A.K.!

¼ cup fine cornmeal, for rolling the dough

1 ball prepared pizza dough, at room temperature

3 tablespoons walnut or other nut oil

1 cup Caramel Sauce (page 165), or store-bought

½ teaspoon fleur de sel or Maldon® sea salt

5 ounces best-available dark or milk chocolate, finely grated

½ cup crushed amaretti cookies

ADVENTURE CLUB Replace the caramel sauce with goat milk caramel (cajeta).

DRINK THIS Nothing is more romantic than rosé champagne.

Preheat the grill per the master instructions for gas (page 11) or charcoal (page 14).

Set a piece of parchment or waxed paper on your work surface. Sprinkle with the cornmeal, then roll out and shape the dough, using a knife if necessary, into a heart shape (per the photo). Place the dough with paper side up on a peel or a rimless baking sheet.

Transfer the dough to your grilling area. Pick up the dough with paper and set down on the grill paper side up. Peel off the paper and grill the first side of the crust per the master instructions on page 11 for gas or page 14 for charcoal until marked and well browned.

Flip the crust and grill on the second side for about 2 minutes, or until golden. When the bottom is marked and browned, use tongs to transfer the crust to a peel or rimless baking sheet. Switch the grill to indirect heat and close the lid to maintain the grill temperature.

Spread the entire surface with caramel sauce, then sprinkle with the salt and chocolate. Finish grilling the pizza, 2 to 4 minutes.

Remove from the grill. Finish with a dusting of crushed amaretti cookies. Slice and serve immediately.

Nibbles & Noshes

In this section, we have strategically designed little nibbles to nosh on before the pizza is served. Think of them as our version of an *amuse bouche*—a little tease for the tummy before the pizza.

Once you get the hang of our nibbles and noshes, add your own versions. Just be sure to follow our credo: create savory, satisfying, and fun-to-eat nibbles that are not predominantly bread or cheese.

Home-Flavored Olives

The south of France and other Mediterranean locales are famous for their many hues of multi-seasoned olives. Besides making a perfect tourist photo, these olives taste as good as they look. We've taken the lead of the olive vendors and created three mixes that comprise our favorite flavors. To make them extra special, warm your olives in the oven or microwave for a few seconds before serving.

Fennel Seed & Orange Zest–Cured Picholine Olives

Makes 2 cups

2	cups picholine (green) olives, drained
1	tablespoon best-quality extra-virgin olive oil
2	tablespoons fennel seeds
	Zest of 1 orange, finely grated with a Microplane or zester
½	teaspoon red pepper flakes (optional)

Toss all the ingredients thoroughly in a bowl and let cure for at least 2 hours, covered but not refrigerated. Refrigerate any unused olives.

They will keep (and get better), tightly covered, for up to 2 weeks in the refrigerator.

Garlic & Red Chile–Cured Black Olives

Makes 2 cups

2	cups Niçoise or Kalamata olives, drained
1	tablespoon best-quality extra-virgin olive oil
3	cloves garlic, minced
	Zest of 1 lemon, finely grated with a Microplane or zester
½	teaspoon dried thyme
1	teaspoon red pepper flakes

Toss all the ingredients thoroughly in a bowl and let cure for at least 2 hours, covered but not refrigerated. Refrigerate any unused olives.

They will keep (and get better), tightly covered, for up to 2 weeks in the refrigerator.

Mixed Olives with Toasted Cumin Seeds

Makes 2 cups

1 tablespoon cumin seeds

2 cups mixed black and green olives such as picholine, Cerignola, Niçoise, Kalamata, or any combination of your favorites, drained

1 tablespoon best-quality extra-virgin olive oil

Zest of 1 lime, finely grated with a Micro-plane or zester

Toast the cumin seeds in a dry skillet over medium-low heat until fragrant, about 4 minutes. Toss all the ingredients thoroughly in a bowl and let cure for at least 2 hours, covered but not refrigerated. Refrigerate any unused olives.

They will keep (and get better), tightly covered, for up to 2 weeks in the refrigerator.

Spiced & Candied Nuts

Call us crazy (and many do), but as with everything we make, we like to take our nuts to the next level. With a few simple ingredients and a minimal amount of effort, these nuts will go from ordinary to superfabulous!

Elizabeth's Famous Sugar & Spice Pecans

Makes 1 pound

⅓ cup firmly packed dark brown sugar

⅔ cup granulated sugar

1 teaspoon kosher salt

¼ teaspoon cayenne pepper

1 teaspoon ground cinnamon

1 large egg white, at room temperature

1 tablespoon water

1 pound pecan halves

Preheat the oven to 300°F.

Mix together the sugars, salt, cayenne, and cinnamon; set aside. In a medium bowl, beat the egg white until frothy but not stiff, add the water, and stir until combined. Add the pecans and stir to coat evenly. Sprinkle with the sugar mixture and stir until evenly coated.

Spread the sugared nuts in a single layer on a cookie sheet fitted with a silicone liner (Silpat®) or parchment paper.

Bake until the sugar coating is crusty and dry, about 30 minutes, stirring occasionally as needed.

Remove from the oven and separate the nuts as they cool. Let cool for at least an hour before serving. These will keep, tightly covered, at room temperature for up to a month, though we guarantee they will disappear long before then!

Tamari Almonds

Makes 1 pound

1	tablespoon toasted sesame oil
3	tablespoons tamari
1	pound whole raw almonds
	Kosher salt to taste

Whisk the oil and tamari together in a medium bowl. Add the almonds and toss to coat. Let sit at room temperature for 1 hour, stirring occasionally.

Preheat the oven to 300°F.

Spread the almonds in a single layer on a cookie sheet fitted with a silicone liner or parchment paper. Bake until the nuts are dry and slightly darker, about 30 minutes, stirring occasionally as needed.

Remove from the oven and immediately season to taste with salt. Let cool for at least an hour before serving. These will keep, tightly covered, at room temperature for up to a month.

Thai Hot Chile–Lime Cashews

Makes 1 pound

¼	cup peanut oil
4	teaspoons Thai garlic chili paste
1	pound raw whole cashews
	Zest of 4 limes, finely grated with a Microplane or zester
¼	cup fresh lime juice (from 2 juicy limes)
¼	cup red pepper flakes
4	teaspoons fine-grain sea salt

Preheat the oven to 300°F.

Mix the peanut oil and chili paste together in a medium sauté pan set over medium heat. Add the cashews, toss thoroughly, and cook for about 2 minutes.

Remove from the heat and spread the cashews in a single layer on a cookie sheet fitted with a silicone liner or parchment paper. Bake until roasted and golden in color, about 15 minutes, stirring a few times as needed.

Remove from the oven, immediately toss with the lime zest and juice, red pepper, and salt. The finished cashews will be a bit wet. Let cool for at least an hour before serving. These will keep, tightly covered, in the refrigerator for up to 3 days.

Note: These addictive cashews will be moist when finished.

Dynamite Dips

The fun thing about dips is that they are slightly retro. But even if dipping isn't the latest, greatest food trend, the proof is in the eatin'—dips are the first thing to disappear at any get-together.

Fire-Roasted Red Pepper Dip

Makes 4 cups

5	red bell Fire-Roasted Peppers (page 167), or store-bought
1	large shallot, roughly chopped
1	head garlic, roasted and squeezed from husks or 2 raw cloves, minced
1	tablespoon olive oil
2	teaspoons fresh lemon juice
1	8-ounce package feta cheese
1	8-ounce package cream cheese
2	teaspoons fresh thyme leaves or ½ teaspoon dried
	Kosher salt and freshly ground black pepper to taste

Place the peppers, shallots, garlic, oil, and lemon juice in a food processor and process until smooth. Add the cheeses and thyme and process again until smooth. Season with salt and pepper.

Refrigerate for a minimum of 3 hours to chill and let the flavors mellow.

The dip will keep, tightly covered, in the refrigerator for up to a week.

Note: To roast garlic, follow the second paragraph of the Roasted Garlic Paste recipe on page 164.

Slow-Roasted Onion Dip

Makes 2½ cups

4	medium Slow-Roasted Onions (page 166)
1	5.2-ounce container boursin cheese
½	cup sour cream
⅛	teaspoon Tabasco sauce
1	teaspoon kosher salt
⅛	teaspoon freshly ground black pepper

Place the onions in a food processor and pulse into a chunky sauce. Add the boursin and pulse until well mixed. Mix in the sour cream by hand. Stir in the Tabasco, salt, and pepper.

Refrigerate for a minimum of 3 hours to chill and let the flavors mellow. Taste and adjust the seasonings if necessary.

The dip will keep, tightly covered, in the refrigerator for up to 3 days.

Grilled Sicilian Caponata

Makes 4 cups

2   large eggplants

1   large zucchini

½   cup olive oil

       Kosher salt to taste

2   medium sweet onions, like Vidalia or Maui, chopped

2   ribs celery, chopped

10   plum tomatoes, peeled, seeded, and diced, or 3 cups canned Italian chopped tomatoes, undrained

1   tablespoon capers, drained

5   tablespoons red-wine vinegar or balsamic vinegar

¼   teaspoon red pepper flakes

½   teaspoon fine-grain sea salt

¼   cup small green olives such as picholine, drained and pitted

       Leaves from 1 bunch fresh basil, chopped just before using

Preheat a gas grill or build a charcoal fire for direct grilling.

Cut the eggplants and zucchini in half lengthwise, then cut the halves lengthwise into slices ½ inch thick. Brush with some of the oil and sprinkle with kosher salt. Place the slices on the cooking grate over direct medium heat and grill until tender and well marked, 3 to 4 minutes per side. Set aside to cool.

Meanwhile, heat enough olive oil to coat the bottom of a large, deep, heavy pot like a Dutch oven or sauté pan over medium heat, then add the onions and celery and cook, stirring occasionally, until golden brown, about 10 minutes. Add the tomatoes, capers, 3 tablespoons of the vinegar, the red pepper, sea salt, and olives and simmer for 15 minutes.

While the tomato mixture is cooking, dice the grilled eggplant and zucchini, then add to the tomatoes and simmer, uncovered, until slightly thickened, another 10 to 15 minutes. Mix the remaining ¼ cup oil and 2 tablespoons vinegar together and stir into the vegetable mixture. Taste and adjust seasonings, adding more vinegar and salt if necessary. Remove from the heat and stir in the basil. Serve warm or cold.

The dip will keep, tightly covered, in the refrigerator for up to 5 days.

Crunchin' Crudités

These colorful raw veggie crudités are a tasty and healthful (shhh!) starter for any party.

Radish Flowers with Sweet Butter & Coarse Salt

Serves 4 to 6

1	bunch radishes, trimmed
¼	cup (½ stick) unsalted butter, softened
2	tablespoons fleur de sel or other fancy salt

To create the "flower" effect, use a paring knife to cut all four sides of the radish (see photo). Place the cut radishes in a bowl of ice water for about 1 hour, until they "bloom" (open).

Just before serving, drain the radishes. To serve, set out the radishes along with individual bowls containing the butter and salt. Instruct guests to take a radish, spread the cut end with butter, and dip in the salt. Devour in one bite—despite what your mother may have taught you.

Steamed Edamame

Serves 4 to 6

1 pound frozen edamame in pods (green soybeans) Kosher salt to taste	Place a steamer basket in a large saucepan filled with 2 inches of water. Add the edamame, cover, and bring the water to a boil. Once the water is boiling, steam until the edamame are tender, about 5 minutes. Remove to a bowl, toss with salt immediately, and serve. We use lots of salt because most of the salt stays on the pod. To eat, simply pop beans out of the pod and enjoy.

Tumbled Tomatoes

Makes 2 pints; serves 4 to 6

1 tablespoon dried herbes de Provence 1 teaspoon coarse sea salt 1 teaspoon dehydrated garlic 2 pints cherry tomatoes	Mix the herbes, salt, and garlic together in a small bowl, then place in a salt grinder or pulverize slightly in a mortar and pestle. If you don't have either, keep the mixture as is. Wash the tomatoes in cold water and drain but do not dry. Place them in a bowl that is large enough so the tomatoes have room to be tumbled. Toss the tomatoes with the herb mixture until they are evenly coated. Refrigerate, uncovered, ideally for several hours, tossing and "tumbling" the tomatoes in the bowl occasionally until all the water is evaporated. Once the water is gone, the herb mixture will form a crust on the tomatoes. They will keep for 2 to 3 days, uncovered, in the refrigerator—if they are not devoured—so make the full recipe and keep them on hand as a healthful snack. Serve chilled.

Mâche & Pomegranate Salad

Serves 4

The tartness of the juice-packed pomegranate seeds plays off the sweetness of the maple syrup–infused dressing to create a perfect fall salad, which, not coincidentally, is when pomegranates are in season.

2   teaspoons balsamic vinegar

1   teaspoon fresh lemon juice

1   tablespoon pure maple syrup

2   teaspoons Dijon mustard

2   teaspoons pomegranate juice (if you are using packaged seeds, get the juice by simply pressing a handful of seeds through a strainer)

3   tablespoons extra-virgin olive oil

4   cups mâche (also called lamb's ear) lettuce or Boston lettuce

¼   cup pomegranate seeds

3   tangerines, supremed (page 181) or, in a pinch, use ¼ cup canned mandarin orange segments

Fleur de sel and freshly ground black pepper to taste

In a large bowl, whisk together the vinegar, lemon juice, maple syrup, and Dijon. Add the pomegranate juice. Drizzle in the oil and whisk until thickened.

Just before serving, add the mâche, pomegranate seeds, and tangerine slices and toss thoroughly with the dressing. Season with salt and pepper and serve.

Fennel, Radicchio & Orange Salad

Serves 4

Fresh, crunchy raw fennel tastes like a cross between licorice and celery. When mixed with bitter radicchio and sweet orange, it hits all your taste buds at once.

2	fennel bulbs
1	small head radicchio
2	teaspoons Dijon mustard
3	tablespoons extra-virgin olive oil
1	tablespoon fresh lemon juice
2	oranges, supremed (page 181), reserve some juice
	Kosher salt and freshly ground black pepper to taste

Trim, core, halve, and slice the fennel bulb into $\frac{1}{8}$-inch-thick strips. Reserve a few of the finer fronds. Core the radicchio and thinly slice.

In a large bowl, whisk together the mustard, oil, lemon juice, and 1 tablespoon orange juice. Add the fennel, radicchio, and supremed orange slices and toss thoroughly. Season with salt and pepper. Top the salad with the reserved fennel fronds and serve.

Super Celery Salad

Serves 4

This simple salad is everything a salad that accompanies a pizza should be: light, refreshing, crispy, and crunchy.

8	ribs of celery heart, ends trimmed
1	2-ounce chunk Parmigiano-Reggiano cheese
$\frac{1}{3}$	cup fresh lemon juice (from 2 to 3 lemons)
$\frac{2}{3}$	cup extra-virgin olive oil
	Kosher salt and freshly ground black pepper to taste

Using a very sharp knife, mandoline, vegetable slicer, or food processor, slice the celery very thinly. Transfer to a large bowl.

With a vegetable peeler, peel off 18 curls of the Parmigiano into a small bowl. Whisk the lemon juice and oil together in a large measuring cup until combined. Season with salt and pepper.

Toss the celery with just enough dressing to coat, and half of the cheese. Top with the remaining cheese. Serve immediately.

Grilled Watermelon Salad

Serves 4

Whoever thought of grilling watermelon? We did! It's unexpected and a real summertime crowd-pleaser. Anyone up for a watermelon seed–spitting contest?!

1   small red or yellow watermelon (3 to 4 pounds), preferably seedless and not too ripe

¼   cup extra-virgin olive oil, plus extra for brushing the melon

3   tablespoons fresh lime juice (about 2 limes)

    Juice of 1 large navel orange

    Pinch of sea or kosher salt, or more to taste

    Pinch of cayenne pepper; or more to taste

¼   cup chopped fresh mint

½   cup crumbled feta cheese (optional)

Preheat a gas grill or build a charcoal fire for direct grilling.

Cut the watermelon in half lengthwise, then cut each half in half. Cut these quarters into 2-inch-thick slices. Brush the slices lightly with olive oil and set aside until ready to grill.

Combine lime and orange juices. Taste; if it is too tart, add more orange juice. It should taste like a "sour" orange. Add the salt and cayenne and whisk continually while adding the oil in a thin stream. Whisk until thickened (emulsified). Taste and adjust the oil and salt to your liking. Add the mint and set aside.

Just before serving, place the oiled watermelon slices on a very clean cooking grate directly over the heat source. Grill until marked and just warmed through but still crunchy, 2 to 3 minutes per side. Let cool.

Cut off the rinds and discard. Cut the watermelon into chunks and place in a serving bowl. Pour the dressing over the top and toss gently. Top with the feta, if desired, and sprinkle with another pinch of cayenne.

Chile-Dusted Jícama & Grapefruit Salad

Serves 4

Crunchy jícama is a staple in the Mexican kitchen. Since it is available year-round, we like to pair it with bright, juicy grapefruit for a winter wonderland salad.

1   medium jícama (about 1 pound)

2   grapefruits (ideally red or pink), supremed (page 181)

¼   cup fresh lime juice (from 2 juicy limes)

Leaves from 3 sprigs fresh cilantro, chopped

Kosher salt to taste

¾   teaspoon ground chipotle or ancho chile (or, in a pinch, cayenne pepper)

With a sharp knife, cut off ½ inch from the top and bottom of the jícama and remove the rest of the peel with a vegetable peeler. Cut the peeled jícama into ½-inch-thick slices, then cut those slices into skinny French fry–like sticks.

Place the jícima and supremed grapefruit slices in a large bowl and toss gently with the lime juice and cilantro. Season with salt and dust with the chile powder. If time permits, chill before serving.

Pickled Cucumber Slices

Serves 4

Less of a salad and more of a palate-cleansing side dish, these bet-you-can't-eat-just-one cucumbers cut the richness of any pizza and are perfect for any of our meatier pizzas.

2   English cucumbers

4   shallots

2   tablespoons sugar

1   tablespoon kosher salt

1   cup cider vinegar

Wash and dry the cucumbers. Peel alternating strips of the green skin off the cucumber with a vegetable peeler. Slice very thin with a mandoline-style slicer, or the slicing disc of a food processor, or a sharp knife. Set aside.

Peel the shallots and slice the same thinness as the cucumbers. In a medium bowl, combine the cucumbers and shallots. The shallot slices will unravel into small rings. Set aside.

In a large measuring cup, whisk together the sugar, salt, and vinegar until completely dissolved. Pour over the salad and mix well, separating the slices to make sure none of them are sticking together. Transfer the salad and all the liquid to a nonreactive metal, plastic, or glass container with a tight lid and refrigerate, turning occasionally, for at least 3 hours and up to 2 days. Serve chilled.

Hong Kong Confetti Salad

Serves 4 to 6

Busy, colorful, and as exciting as a Hong Kong night.

2   tablespoons sesame seeds

¼   cup unseasoned rice vinegar

2   teaspoons toasted sesame oil

2   teaspoons fresh lime juice (about ½ lime)

1   tablespoon honey

1½   tablespoons peeled and finely grated
     fresh ginger

¼   teaspoon cayenne pepper

2   medium carrots, shredded

½   small head red cabbage, cored, then cut
     crosswise into the narrowest ribbons
     possible and separated

1   yellow bell pepper, seeded and cut length-
     wise into the thinnest strips possible

1   red bell pepper, seeded and cut lengthwise
     into the thinnest strips possible

½   medium sweet onion, thinly sliced and
     separated into rings

½   cup chopped lightly packed fresh cilantro
     leaves

Toast the sesame seeds in a dry skillet over medium heat until golden brown, about 2 minutes. Set aside to cool.

In a small bowl, whisk together the vinegar, oil, lime juice, honey, ginger, and cayenne. Set aside.

In a large bowl, combine the carrots, cabbage, bell peppers, onions, and cilantro and toss thoroughly. Toss with the dressing to coat well, then garnish with the sesame seeds. Serve immediately.

Note: If preparing more than an hour in advance, keep the cabbage separate and dress the salad just before serving (otherwise the whole salad will be purple).

The Pantry

Our pizza pantry is full of the recipes for the basic sauces and toppings that you need to make our pizzas. If you keep your pizza pantry full, you will be able to whip together crowd-pleasing pizzas, or an easy meal for one, any night of the week.

Basic Pizza Dough—Handmade

This is a basic white pizza dough; to make whole wheat dough, use a combination of whole wheat and white bread flour. The best ratio is 25 percent whole grain flour and 75 percent all-purpose flour. If you use too much whole grain flour, the crust will be leaden, not light and airy.

Makes enough for 2 pizza crusts

1   cup lukewarm water, plus extra as needed

¼   cup olive oil, plus extra for oiling the bowl

1   teaspoon sugar or honey

1   package active dry yeast (2¼ teaspoons)

3   cups unbleached all-purpose flour, plus extra as needed

¼   teaspoon kosher salt

Place the water, oil, and sugar in a large bowl. Sprinkle the yeast on top and let sit until foamy, about 5 minutes.

In a medium bowl, combine the flour and salt. Add to the water mixture, ½ cup at a time, until well incorporated. If the dough is stiff, add more water. If it is very sticky, add extra flour, 1 tablespoon at a time, until the dough is soft and slightly sticky. Continue to mix until it feels elastic. Turn the dough out onto a well-floured work surface. Knead for about 1 minute, until just smooth and easy to work with, adding extra flour to the surface as necessary to prevent the dough from sticking. Do not overwork the dough or it will be tough.

Place the dough in an oiled clean bowl, turn it several times to coat all over with the oil, then drizzle the top of the dough with a little oil. Cover tightly with plastic wrap, place in a warm spot, and let rise until it more than doubles in volume, about 1 hour.

Punch the dough down and knead on a lightly floured surface for 1 to 2 minutes, until smooth. Divide into two equal-size balls and proceed with your pizza making. (The dough may be made ahead, frozen for up to a month, and thawed at room temperature before using.)

Basic Pizza Dough—By Machine

This recipe is so fast that you can start it when you get home from work and be grilling your pizza 30 minutes later. It can be made in a stand mixer fitted with the dough hook attachment or in a food processor.

Makes enough for 2 pizza crusts

1 cup lukewarm water

¼ cup olive oil, plus extra for oiling bowl

1½ teaspoons sugar or honey

1 package rapid-rise yeast (2¼ teaspoons)

3 cups bread flour or all-purpose flour, plus extra as needed

1½ teaspoons kosher salt

If your kitchen is cool, preheat the oven to 150°F or the lowest setting.

Pour the water into the work bowl of a large food processor or stand mixer. Sprinkle the oil, sugar, and yeast over the water and pulse several times until mixed. Add the flour and salt and process until the mixture comes together. The dough should be soft and slightly sticky. (If it is very sticky, add flour, 1 tablespoon at a time, and pulse until smooth. If it is too stiff, add water, 1 tablespoon at a time, and pulse until smooth.)

Turn the dough onto a lightly floured work surface; knead by hand to form a smooth, round ball. Put the dough in an oiled clean bowl, turn it over several times in the bowl to coat it with oil, drizzle a little oil over the top, and cover tightly with plastic wrap. Place in a warm spot or turn off the oven and stick it in there. Let rise until the dough has doubled in size, about 15 minutes in the oven or 1 hour in the warm spot.

Once the dough has risen, punch it down and knead on a lightly floured surface for 1 to 2 minutes, until smooth. Divide into two equal-size balls and proceed with your pizza making. (The dough may be made ahead, frozen for up to a month, and thawed at room temperature before using.)

Artisanal Baker´s Dough

In the infancy of our grilled pizza days, we were thrilled with the results of pizzas made with store-bought or pizzeria-bought dough. We still love it, but now that we have become dough snobs, we appreciate the subtle nuances of this 24-hour "aged" artisanal dough. Of all the doughs, it takes the least amount of time and effort to prepare. The only drawback is that it has to be made 24 hours in advance. When time permits, it's unquestionably our favorite dough option.

Makes enough for 2 pizza crusts

3   cups bread flour or all-purpose flour

½   teaspoon active dry yeast

¾   teaspoon kosher salt

1¼   cups 2% milk

2   tablespoons olive oil, plus more for bowl

Whisk the flour, yeast, and salt together in a large bowl, then pour in the milk and oil. Mix together with a large fork or your hands. Knead once or twice to form a ball. It may be sticky, but that's okay.

Oil a bowl and set the dough in it. Lay a sheet of waxed paper loosely over the top, then cover with plastic wrap. Place a clean dish towel over the bowl and allow to rise at room temperature and undisturbed for 24 hours. Turn the dough once in the bowl about 3 hours before you want to use it. The 24-hour fermentation process takes the place of kneading the dough.

When you are ready to make your pizza, divide the dough in half on a lightly floured board, then proceed with your pizza making. (The dough can be frozen for up to a month; thaw at room temperature before using.)

Sweet Pizza Doughs

When making dessert pizzas, we thought it would be fun to experiment with sweet-flavored pizza dough. When we tried to knead cinnamon sugar and chocolate chips into the dough, the taste was great but it didn't give it the texture we were looking for. To solve this problem, add a touch of sugar and the flavorings to the flour before adding any of the wet ingredients.

CHOCOLATE DOUGH

Add 2 tablespoons sugar and ¼ cup unsweetened cocoa powder to the flour. Stir and follow the recipe as written above.

CINNAMON DOUGH

Add 2 tablespoons sugar and 4 teaspoons ground cinnamon to the flour. Stir and follow the recipe as written above. Feel free to substitute these doughs for any of the sweeter pizzas.

Spelt Dough

Our spelt* dough has a sweet, nutty whole wheat flavor that is instantly pleasing. But because of the properties of spelt, it will never stretch or rise like conventional pizza dough. Spelt flour can be purchased at most large grocery and health-food stores.

Makes enough for 2 pizza crusts

1   cup lukewarm water

1   tablespoon honey

1   package active dry yeast (2¼ teaspoons)

3   cups spelt flour

1   teaspoon fine-grain sea salt

2   tablespoons olive oil

Pour the water into a large bowl, then add the honey and yeast. In a medium bowl, combine the flour and salt. When the yeast begins to foam, mix in 1 cup of the flour. Add the oil and mix until completely incorporated. Add the remaining flour ¼ cup at a time, mixing well with your hands or a fork.

Sprinkle a little flour on your work surface, turn out the dough, and knead until it feels smooth. The dough should be soft and slightly sticky. (If it is very sticky, add flour, 1 tablespoon at a time, and mix until smooth. If it is too stiff, add water, 1 tablespoon at a time, and mix until smooth.)

Form the dough into a ball and place in an oiled clean bowl. Drizzle a little oil over the top and make sure it is evenly coated with the oil. Cover with plastic wrap and a clean dish towel and set aside in a warm spot. Let rise until it has doubled in size, about 1 hour.

When you are ready to make your pizza, divide the dough in two on a lightly floured board and proceed with your pizza making. (The dough can be frozen for up to a month; thaw at room temperature before using.)

*Many people who have trouble digesting regular wheat are able to tolerate spelt. However, we do not encourage those with wheat sensitivities to consume this grain because it is a member of the wheat family.

Gluten-Free Pizza Dough

Makes 1 ball of dough, enough for one 12-inch pizza crust

¾ cup lukewarm water (70° to 95°F) + extra as needed

2 tablespoons olive oil + extra for oiling the pan

1 teaspoon sugar

1 package active dry yeast (2¼ teaspoons)

1½ cups C4C Gluten-Free Flour Mix or King Arthur Gluten-Free Multi-Purpose Flour + extra as needed

1 teaspoon xanthan gum

1 teaspoon baking powder

½ teaspoon kosher salt

1 egg yolk

2 tablespoons grits or polenta

Notes:

- You may find it helpful to cut the cooled pizza crust in half for storage.

- Xanthan gum comes in powder form and 8 ounces costs about $15. One package will last you for ages. It's available at most specialty stores and many grocery stores.

- We find it efficient to par-bake multiple crusts at once and freeze them individually so that they are at the ready anytime the craving for grilled pizza hits.

In a medium bowl, combine the water, oil, and sugar. Sprinkle the yeast on top and let sit until foamy, about 5 minutes.

In a large bowl, add the flour, xanthan gum, baking powder, and salt. Mix well.

Add the egg yolk to the liquid/yeast mixture and beat until combined. Add the wet mixture to the dry mixture and blend with a fork until well incorporated and the dough has the feel of slightly sticky conventional dough. Do not overwork. If the dough is too dry, add additional water, 1 tablespoon at a time. If it is very sticky, add additional flour, 1 tablespoon at a time.

Generously oil a rimless baking sheet (or turn a rimmed cookie sheet upside down and use the bottom), and sprinkle with 1 tablespoon polenta. Use your hands and/or a well-oiled rolling pin to create a ⅛ to ¼-inch-thick crust in the center of the pan (⅛ inch is ideal). Sprinkle the remaining polenta over top of the dough. Cover the dough with plastic wrap and place in a warm area. After 30 minutes you should see a significant rise in the dough. Let the dough rise for another 30 minutes (an hour in total), or until almost doubled in thickness.

Preheat the oven to 350°F. Remove the plastic and par-bake the dough for 10 minutes. The dough should be cooked through, but not browned. Par-baked dough can be grilled immediately, refrigerated for up to 2 days in a resealable plastic bag, or frozen for later use.

Tomato-Basil Base

Makes 4 cups

2 pints cherry tomatoes, quartered, or 2 pounds vine-ripened or heirloom tomatoes, diced

2 tablespoons olive oil

1 tablespoon balsamic vinegar

1 teaspoon kosher salt

5 cloves garlic, minced

5 large fresh basil leaves, chopped just before using

Mix together all the ingredients, except the basil, in a medium nonreactive metal or glass bowl. If serving within 1 to 2 hours, let stand at room temperature so the tomatoes release their juices, or refrigerate, covered, up to 24 hours.

Mix and drain the excess juice from the tomatoes. If refrigerated, bring to room temperature. Just before using, stir in the basil.

Tuscan Red Sauce

Makes about 2½ cups

2 pounds (about 10) plum tomatoes

5 fresh sage leaves

1 teaspoon kosher salt

4 cloves garlic, roughly chopped

1 tablespoon extra-virgin olive oil, or more to taste

Place a 4- or 5-quart saucepan on the stove. Break each tomato open by squeezing it with your hand over the saucepan. Once each tomato is cracked, place it in the pan. Add the sage, salt, and garlic and cover.

Cook over medium heat for 45 to 60 minutes, stirring occasionally. The tomatoes will break down and liquefy as they cook. When the tomatoes are thick and saucy (about the texture of ketchup), remove from the heat. Let cool to room temperature.

Process the sauce through a food mill or strainer to remove the seeds and skins, then adjust the seasonings. Whisk in the oil.

Crushed Tomato Sauce

Makes 1½ cups

1   14.5-ounce can crushed tomatoes with or without basil, undrained

1   clove garlic, minced

Sea salt and freshly ground black pepper to taste

Pour the crushed tomatoes into a small nonreactive metal or glass bowl. Add the garlic and season with salt and pepper. Drain the excess liquid from the tomatoes and discard.

Note: If you cannot find crushed tomatoes, pour a can of stewed plum tomatoes into a food mill, blender, or food processor and purée.

Five-Minute Amatrici-Style Sauce

Makes 3 cups

8   strips center-cut bacon (ideally Nueske's pepper-crusted smoked bacon), chopped

2   tablespoons extra-virgin olive oil

1   14.5-ounce can chopped tomatoes, any flavor, undrained

1   clove garlic, minced or grated

½   teaspoon red pepper flakes

Sea salt and freshly ground black pepper to taste

Preheat an 8-inch skillet over medium-high heat for 1 to 2 minutes. Add the bacon and a little of the oil and cook, stirring, to brown the bits and render the fat.

Add the tomatoes and cook, stirring, until warmed through, then add the garlic, red pepper, and the rest of the oil. Simmer for another minute, then remove from the heat.

Season with salt and black pepper and cool before using. This will keep, tightly covered, in the refrigerator for up to 3 days.

Basil Pesto

Makes 1½ cups

---

1   cup pine nuts or walnuts, lightly toasted (page 181)

4   cups fresh basil leaves

⅔   cup freshly grated Parmigiano-Reggiano cheese

4   cloves garlic, minced

¾   cup olive oil

¼   teaspoon kosher salt

¼   teaspoon freshly ground black pepper

Place all the ingredients in a food processor and process until smooth. Taste and adjust the salt and pepper, if necessary.

This will keep, tightly covered, in the refrigerator for up to 3 days or in the freezer for up to 2 months.

Sun-Dried Tomato Pesto

Makes about 2½ cups

¼   cup chopped walnuts, lightly toasted (page 181)

½   cup fresh basil leaves

⅔   cup freshly grated Parmigiano-Reggiano cheese

1   clove garlic, minced

1   cup oil-packed sun-dried tomatoes (one 8.5-ounce jar), plus ⅓ cup of the oil (top off with olive oil if necessary)

⅔   cup olive oil

¼   teaspoon kosher salt

¼   teaspoon freshly ground black pepper

Place all the ingredients in a food processor and process until smooth. Taste and adjust the salt and pepper, if necessary.

This will keep, tightly covered, in the refrigerator for up to 3 days or in the freezer for up to 2 months.

White Bean Purée

Makes 3 cups

2	15-ounce cans white beans (cannellini or Great Northern)
1	cup water
3	cloves garlic, cut in half
1	sprig fresh rosemary
¼	cup olive oil
1	head garlic, roasted (page 164)
2	teaspoons chopped fresh rosemary
	Kosher salt and white pepper to taste

Drain and rinse the beans and set aside. Place the water, fresh garlic, and whole sprig of rosemary in a medium saucepan. Bring to a boil, add the beans, and simmer for 3 to 4 minutes. Drain, reserving the bean cooking water. Remove the rosemary sprig.

Place the beans and boiled garlic in a food processor. Add a couple tablespoons of the bean water to thin out the consistency and process until smooth. Then add 3 tablespoons of the oil, the roasted garlic, and chopped rosemary and purée again. Taste and add more oil if necessary. Season with salt and pepper. Let cool.

This will keep, tightly covered, in the refrigerator for up to 3 days. Use any leftovers as a dip and serve with pita chips and crudités.

Grilled Eggplant Purée

Makes about 2 cups

2	large or 3 medium eggplants
⅓	cup olive oil
½	teaspoon kosher salt
½	teaspoon freshly ground black pepper

Preheat a gas grill or build a charcoal fire.

Place the whole eggplants on the cooking grate over direct medium-high heat. Grill, rotating every 5 minutes, until all of the skin is blackened to a crisp and the eggplants have collapsed and shrunken in size by approximately one-half, about 30 minutes.

When cool enough to handle, slice the eggplants in half and remove the pulp from the skin. Discard the skin and save any of the juices. Place the pulp and juices in a bowl. Use a large fork to mash the eggplant, then blend in the oil, salt, and pepper.

This will keep, tightly covered, in the refrigerator for up to 3 days.

Black Olive Purée (Tapenade)

Makes 2 cups

2 cups Kalamata olives, drained and pitted (discard any mushy olives)

Finely grated zest and juice of 1 lemon

2 cloves garlic, minced

⅛ teaspoon red pepper flakes

½ teaspoon freshly ground black pepper

½ cup lightly packed fresh Italian parsley leaves

2 tablespoons olive oil

Place all the ingredients in a food processor and process until smooth.

This will keep, tightly covered, in the refrigerator for up to 3 days.

Note: Other types of black olives may be used, but stay away from the common colossal black olive.

Artichoke Spread

Makes 3 cups

1 cup best-quality mayonnaise

2 14-ounce cans water- or brine-packed artichoke hearts, drained

1 cup freshly grated Parmigiano-Reggiano cheese

½ cup grated pecorino romano cheese

1 tablespoon Dijon mustard

½ teaspoon Worcestershire sauce

1 tablespoon fresh thyme leaves

⅛ teaspoon freshly ground white pepper

Preheat the oven to 350°F.

Combine the mayonnaise, artichokes, cheeses, mustard, Worcestershire, thyme, and pepper.

Mash together using the back of a fork until well mixed and the artichokes are in smaller pieces. Put in an ovenproof dish, cover with aluminum foil, and bake until bubbly, about 30 minutes. Let cool before using.

This will keep, tightly covered, in the refrigerator for up to 2 days. You can rebake and serve any left-over spread with pita chips as a dip.

Hummin' Hummus

Makes 1½ cups

1   15-ounce can chickpeas (garbanzo beans), drained and rinsed well

3   tablespoons fresh lemon juice (from about 2 lemons)

3   cloves garlic, very finely minced

⅓   cup tahini (sesame seed paste)

¼   teaspoon cayenne pepper

¼   teaspoon kosher salt

¼   cup olive oil

Place all the ingredients in a food processor and process until smooth. Taste and adjust the salt, if necessary.

This will keep, tightly covered, in the refrigerator for up to 2 days.

Roasted Garlic Paste

Makes about ½ cup, enough for 1 pizza

3   heads garlic

3   tablespoons olive oil, plus extra for drizzling

Kosher salt

Preheat the oven to 400°F.

Remove the first layer of papery skin from the garlic. Slice off ¼ inch from the pointy top. Place each head on a sheet of aluminum foil, cut side up. Drizzle with the oil and season with salt. Wrap each head in the foil and roast until the cloves are golden brown and soft, about 1 hour. Remove from the heat and let cool. (You can also do this on the grill, cooking over indirect heat.)

Remove the roasted cloves from their skins. The most efficient way to do this is to squeeze the whole head from the bottom. Using a fork, vigorously mix the garlic and oil together. Add a pinch of salt. (If your recipe calls for just a clove or two of roasted garlic, you can remove it from the skin using a small escargot-style fork.)

This will keep, tightly covered, in the refrigerator for up to 2 days.

Chocolate Ganache

Makes 1 cup

⅓ cup heavy or whipping cream

2 tablespoons superfine sugar

6 ounces bittersweet chocolate

1 tablespoon bourbon or a sweet liqueur (optional)

1 teaspoon vanilla extract

Pinch of sea salt

In a small saucepan, heat the cream over medium heat to almost boiling, then add the sugar and stir to combine.

Meanwhile, place the chocolate in a medium bowl. Remove the cream from the heat and pour over the chocolate. Whisk vigorously until it's melted and well combined. Add the bourbon, vanilla, and salt, stirring constantly until the mixture is cool the touch. If the chocolate does not melt all the way, place the mixture in a double boiler and gently heat until melted.

This will keep, tightly covered, in the refrigerator for up to a week.

Caramel Sauce

Makes about 1 cup

1 cup sugar

2 tablespoons water

1 cup heavy cream

¼ teaspoon vanilla extract

Pinch of fleur de sel or best available salt

Combine the sugar and water in a medium saucepan (ideally a tall 1½-quart pan). Cook over medium heat, without stirring, until the sugar melts and turns golden brown, about 5 minutes. (Keep a watchful eye on the sugar because it can burn quickly.)

Immediately remove from the heat and whisk in the cream, vanilla, and fleur de sel until smooth. (Note: When adding and stirring the cream, wear an oven mitt on your stirring hand. The heat of the sugar will create a tremendous amount of scalding steam when it comes into contact with the cream.) At this point, the sauce will be very thin. After it cools, it will thicken to the consistency of, well, caramel sauce.

This will keep, tightly covered, in the refrigerator for up to a week.

Slow-Roasted Onions

Makes 4 roasted onions

4	medium sweet onions, like Vidalia or Maui
2	teaspoons olive oil
	Fleur de sel or coarse sea salt to taste

Preheat the oven to 325°F, or preheat a gas grill or build a charcoal fire.

Leaving the skins on the onions, rub them lightly with the oil and place on the cooking grate of the grill over indirect medium heat or on a baking sheet in the oven. Grill or roast for 1½ to 2 hours, depending on their size. Check the onions periodically and remove when you can see the dark onion juices bursting through the skins. When cool enough to touch, remove the skins and sprinkle with salt.

These will keep, tightly covered, in the refrigerator for up to 2 days.

Note: This can be done with any onion, including shallots.

Onion Marmalade

Makes 1 cup, enough for 1 pizza

2	tablespoons olive oil
1	tablespoon unsalted butter (or salted and reduce the salt a bit)
3	large yellow onions, thinly sliced and roughly separated into rings
1	teaspoon kosher salt

Heat the oil and butter together in a large, heavy sauté pan over medium heat. When the butter bubbles, add the onion rings and salt and cook, covered, for 20 minutes, stirring occasionally. Remove the cover and cook, stirring occasionally, until the onions are all a deep golden color, about 20 more minutes.

This will keep, tightly covered, in the refrigerator for up to 2 days.

Fire-Roasted Peppers

Makes ½ cup strips (poblanos slightly less), enough for 1 pizza

2 bell peppers or poblanos	Preheat a gas grill or build a charcoal fire.
	
	    Place the peppers on the cooking grate over direct high heat. Turn occasionally until the skins are blackened and blistered all over, about 15 minutes. Immediately put in a paper bag or sealed plastic container until cool to the touch. Slip the skins off and seed the peppers. Cut into strips.
	
	    These will keep, tightly covered, in the refrigerator for up to 3 days.

Fire-Roasted Cherry Tomatoes

Makes 40 tomatoes

40   cherry tomatoes (we like those sold on the vine)
 	
1   teaspoon olive oil or as needed to coat
 	
1   cup kosher salt
	Preheat a gas grill, build a charcoal fire, or preheat the oven to 275°F.
	
	    Lightly coat the tomatoes with the oil. Cover a rimmed baking sheet with the salt to form a "salt bed." Place the tomatoes closely together bottom side down on the salt bed. Place the baking sheet on the grill on the cooking grate over low indirect heat or in the oven. Slowly roast until the tomatoes are shriveled and soft, about 2 hours. Remove from the grill or oven and let cool.
	
	    They will keep, tightly covered, in the refrigerator for up to 2 days.

Walnut Spread

Makes about 1½ cups

1   pound (2 cups) walnut halves or pieces, toasted (page 181)

3   tablespoons granulated sugar

2   tablespoons pure maple syrup

2   tablespoons walnut oil

     Pinch of kosher salt; more to taste

In a food processor, combine the toasted walnuts, 2 tablespoons of the granulated sugar, the maple syrup, 2 tablespoons walnut oil, and a pinch of salt, then process until the texture resembles peanut butter. Reserve 1 cup of it for topping and refrigerate the rest in an airtight container, where it will keep for 1 week.

Beer Can Chicken

Makes about 4 cups chopped chicken

1   4- to 5-pound roasting chicken

1   tablespoon olive oil

     Kosher salt and freshly ground black pepper to taste

1   12-ounce can beer

Preheat a gas grill, build a charcoal fire, or preheat the oven to 350°F.

Remove the neck and giblets and if desired, rinse the chicken inside and out; pat dry with paper towels. Coat the chicken lightly with the oil and season with salt and pepper.

Open the beer can and drink (or discard) a third of the beer. Place the can on a counter and pick up the chicken with both hands. Slide it over the beer can so that it appears to be "sitting" on the beer can like a throne. If cooking in the oven, place the beer-roosted chicken in a small cake pan, making

sure the drumsticks are in front of the can—this will keep the chicken stable. If grilling, place the chicken-on-a-can on the cooking grate, away from the heat source, making sure the drumsticks are in front of the chicken—like a tripod.

Cook the chicken, with the lid down, until the juices run clear and an instant-read thermometer inserted in the thickest part of the thigh registers 180°F and 160°F in the breast, about 1¼ hours. If cooking with charcoal, you will need to add more briquettes after 45 to 60 minutes to maintain the heat level. Remove from the oven or grill and let rest for 10 minutes before carving. Leftovers will keep, tightly covered, in the refrigerator for up to 2 days.

Note: When removing the chicken from the grate, be careful not to spill the contents of the beer can, as it will be very hot.

Caesar Salad Dressing

Makes ½ cup

1   egg

¼   teaspoon kosher salt

1   teaspoon coarsely ground black pepper

4   cloves garlic, minced

2   anchovy fillets or 1 heaping teaspoon anchovy paste

2   teaspoons Dijon mustard

1½   tablespoons fresh lemon juice

1   teaspoon Worcestershire sauce

1½   teaspoons red-wine vinegar

¼   cup safflower or olive oil

Before making the dressing, fill a small pot with cold water and bring to a boil. Add the egg in the shell, turn off heat, and cook for 2 minutes. Separate the egg and discard the white.

Combine the salt, pepper, garlic, anchovies, Dijon, lemon juice, Worcestershire, and vinegar in a blender and process until smooth. Add the oil and pulse a few times. Add the coddled yolk and pulse a couple more times—just enough to blend it without causing the dressing to become like mayonnaise.

This will keep, tightly covered, in the refrigerator for up to 2 days.

Chimichurri Sauce

Makes about 1 cup

3   cups lightly packed chopped fresh parsley, stems removed

2   cloves garlic, minced

¼   teaspoon red pepper flakes

2   tablespoons minced shallot or onion

½   cup olive oil

1   tablespoon sherry vinegar or red-wine vinegar

1   tablespoon fresh lemon juice

     Kosher salt and freshly ground black pepper to taste

In a food processor or blender, combine the parsley, minced garlic, red pepper flakes, shallots, olive oil, vinegar, lemon juice, and salt and pepper to taste. Pulse until well chopped, but not puréed. Reserve for topping. It will keep, tightly covered, in the refrigerator for up to 2 days.

North Carolina–Style Pulled Pork

Makes 4 pounds cooked meat

Hickory wood chips, soaked in water for 30 minutes and drained right before using

1   7- to 9-pound pork butt

Olive oil for brushing pork

1   teaspoon kosher salt

2   teaspoons freshly ground black pepper

Carolina Vinegar Sauce (facing page)

Carolina Coleslaw (facing page)

Preheat a gas grill or build a charcoal fire.

Before placing the meat on the grill, add the soaked wood chips directly to the white-gray ash briquettes or the smoking box of your gas grill. If using charcoal, you will need to add more every hour to maintain the heat level.

Don't trim any excess fat off the meat; this fat will naturally baste the meat and keep it moist during the long cooking time. Brush the pork with a thin coating of oil. Season with the salt and pepper.

Place the pork on the cooking grate, fat side up, away from the heat source. Cook, with the lid down, maintaining a temperature in the grill of 325° to 350°F, until an instant-read thermometer inserted into the middle of the pork registers 190° to 200°F, 4 to 5 hours. There is no need to turn the meat dur-

ing the entire cooking time. The meat should be very tender and falling apart. If there is a bone, it should come out smoothly, with no meat clinging to it. (This is the real test for doneness on the barbecue circuit.)

Let the meat rest until cool enough to handle, about 20 minutes. Using rubber food-service gloves, pull the meat from the skin, bones, and fat. Set aside any crispy bits (fat) that have been completely rendered and look almost burned. Working quickly, shred the chunks of meat by crossing two forks and "pulling" the meat into small pieces from the roast. Chop the reserved crispy bits and mix it into the pulled pork. While the meat is still warm, mix with enough vinegar sauce to moisten and season the meat, about 1 cup. The recipe can be made in advance up to this point and reheated with about ½ cup additional sauce in a double boiler. This will keep, tightly covered, in the refrigerator for up to 3 days and in the freezer for up to a month.

Note: If you're lucky enough to live near a great barbecue joint, buy their pulled pork. If not, make this for your next cookout and save 1 cup for each pulled pork pizza you want to make—it's the ultimate grilled-over!

Carolina Vinegar Sauce

Makes 2½ cups

2 cups cider vinegar

½ cup ketchup

1 tablespoon kosher salt

1 tablespoon ground white pepper

1 tablespoon red pepper flakes

2 tablespoons granulated sugar

¼ cup dark firmly packed dark brown sugar

½ teaspoon freshly ground black pepper

Mix all the ingredients together and let sit for at least 10 minutes before using.

This will keep, tightly covered, in the refrigerator for up to a week.

Note: The longer this sauce sits, the hotter it gets since the heat from the red pepper flakes is brought out by the vinegar. Start with 1 tablespoon red pepper flakes, then add more to taste.

Carolina Coleslaw

Makes 4 cups

1 recipe Carolina Vinegar Sauce (recipe above)

1 medium head green cabbage, cored and chopped

In a large bowl, combine the sauce and cabbage until well mixed and not quite wet. Cover with plastic wrap and refrigerate for at least 2 hours or overnight.

This will keep, tightly covered, in the refrigerator for up to 2 days.

Sweet Potato Bourbon Mash

Makes about 2 cups

2	large sweet potatoes, preferably Garnet (dark-red-skinned)
⅓	cup heavy cream
1	ounce bourbon (make mine a Maker's Mark® please!)
2	tablespoons dark brown sugar
⅛	teaspoon kosher salt
1	dash Tabasco
1	pinch freshly grated nutmeg (optional)

Prick the potatoes with a fork. Roast on the grill over indirect heat, or in a 400°F oven for 1 hour, or until sugar beads start to form on the skin. Let cool to the touch, then peel the potatoes and cut them into quarters. Place the potatoes in a small saucepan, and add the cream, bourbon, sugar, and salt. Mash the potatoes with a large fork and blend the ingredients together along with ⅓ cup water. Stir until smooth.

Simmer, covered, over medium-low heat for 15 to 20 minutes, or until the potatoes are so soft that they resemble a purée. When the potatoes have cooked down, add the Tabasco and nutmeg. Taste and adjust the salt as necessary.

"You are SO Chopped Liver" Paté

Makes about 2 cups (send your kids to school with leftover chicken liver sandwiches!)

1	pound chicken livers
2	tablespoons unsalted butter
2	shallots, diced
½	teaspoon kosher salt
¼	teaspoon allspice (optional)
¼	teaspoon freshly ground black pepper
1	teaspoon fresh thyme leaves or ¼ teaspoon dried thyme
1	ounce brandy or cognac

Rinse the chicken livers in cold water and clean any fat and sinew.

Preheat a heavy sauté or saucepan over medium-high heat, and melt the butter. Add the shallots and salt and sauté until they begin to brown. Add the livers, allspice, pepper, and thyme and cook for approximately 10 minutes, or until the livers are cooked but still slightly pink inside.

While the liver mixture is still warm, transfer the pan contents to a food processor; add the brandy or cognac and purée until smooth. Refrigerate until firm.

Note: This is best made the day before so that the ingredients have a chance to kibbitz.

Popcorn Chicken

Makes enough for 1 pizza plus a few treats for the cook!

1   cup buttermilk

1   tablespoon hot sauce

2   boneless chicken breasts, cut into ½-inch cubes

1   cup all-purpose or gluten-free flour

2   teaspoons kosher salt

1   teaspoon freshly grated black pepper

¼   teaspoon cayenne

4   whole eggs

2   tablespoons milk

¼   teaspoon sea salt

¼   teaspoon white pepper

2-3 cups panko

    Peanut oil for frying

In a large bowl, combine the buttermilk and hot sauce; add the chicken and marinate for 15 minutes. Drain. In another large bowl, mix the flour, kosher salt, black pepper, and cayenne. Coat pieces of chicken in the flour and set on a rack. Let sit for 5 minutes. Meanwhile make the egg wash by beating the eggs, milk, sea salt, and white pepper together.

Place the panko in a large bowl. Coat each piece of chicken individually with the egg wash and roll in the panko. Place back on the rack and let sit for 5 minutes before frying.

Pour enough oil into a small, tall, heavy-bottomed pot until it is 3 inches deep. Heat the oil until it reaches 350°F.

When the oil is ready, fry a third of the chicken pieces for 5 minutes, or until cooked throughout and nicely browned. Reserve on a piece of paper towel and continue frying the remaining two batches.

Notes:

- If you don't have an oil or candy thermometer, stick a ½-inch cube of bread on a fork or skewer and dip it in the oil. If the oil bubbles but the bread doesn't brown after 10 seconds, the oil is not hot enough. If the bread browns instantly, the oil temperature is too high. And if the bread turns into a golden crouton in 5 to 10 seconds, you are set to fry,

- Hot oil is very dangerous. Never leave it unattended on the stove. And don't start drinking until after you have finished frying. The best way to put out an oil fire is to smother it with a tightly fitting lid. Or run a cloth under the tap, wring it out, and use it to cover the flaming pan. Never throw water over burning oil, and never attempt to move a burning pan.

Marsala Meatballs

Makes about 15 mini meatballs, enough for 1 large pizza

Olive oil for the sautéing mushrooms and shallots and oiling the pan

1 pound mushrooms, cleaned and sliced

1 shallot, chopped and sautéed

1 pound ground veal

2 cloves of garlic, grated

1 teaspoon chopped fresh parsley

1 tablespoon chopped fresh thyme leaves

¼ cup grated pecorino cheese

¼ cup marsala wine

1 large egg, mixed

¼ cup matzoh or saltine crackers, crushed (gluten-free or regular)

1 teaspoon sea salt

In a medium pan, heat about 2 tablespoons of olive oil and sauté the sliced mushrooms and shallots until cooked through. Chop the mushrooms and reserve.

Preheat the oven to 350°F. Drizzle about a tablespoon of the olive oil into a 9x13-inch baking dish and distribute to evenly coat the entire surface. Set aside.

Combine the ground veal, sautéed mushroom mixture, garlic, parsley, and thyme in a large mixing bowl and mix by hand until thoroughly incorporated.

Mix the cheese, wine, eggs, cracker crumbs, and salt together. Add gradually to the meatball mixture and mix to combine. Do not overmix! Roll the mixture into round, golf ball–size meatballs (about 1½ inches), making sure to pack the meat firmly. Place the balls in the prepared baking dish, being careful to line them up snugly and in even rows vertically and horizontally to form a grid. The meatballs should be touching one another.

Roast for 20 minutes, or until the meatballs are firm and cooked through. A meat thermometer inserted into the center of a meatball should read 165°F.

Allow the meatballs to cool for 5 minutes in the baking dish before serving.

Pimiento Cheese

Makes about 1¼ cups

12 ounces extra-sharp Cheddar cheese, grated by hand

¼ cup best-quality mayonnaise, such as Hellmann's

2 tablespoons cream cheese, room temperature

¼ cup (2-ounce jar) diced Dromedary® pimientos

Freshly ground black pepper

In a medium bowl mix the cheese and mayonnaise together with a fork until it holds together. Add the cream cheese and pimientos and mix to distribute. Season with a generous amount of freshly ground black pepper.

Cover and refrigerate until ready to serve. Reserve for the pizza or serve with celery sticks, crackers, or even in a sandwich.

Pistachio Pesto with Mint

Makes about ¾ cup

6 tablespoons olive oil + more as needed

½ cup shelled pistachios

1 lightly packed cup fresh mint leaves, stems discarded

½ cup grated Parmigiano-Reggiano

Zest of 1 orange

1 clove garlic

¼ teaspoon freshly ground black pepper

Combine all the ingredients in a food processor fitted with a steel blade. Pulse to mix and purée. Add more olive oil if necessary to make it easier to spread.

Hot Pepper Jelly Glaze

Makes 1⅓ cups; use extra as a glaze on meat, poultry, or vegetables

1   12-ounce jar of store-bought or homemade hot pepper jelly (see page 179)

2   tablespoons unseasoned rice vinegar + more as needed

Pinch of crushed red pepper flakes (optional)

Pinch of kosher salt

Place the contents of a jar of hot pepper jelly into a small heavy-bottomed saucepan set over low heat. Melt the jelly, stirring occasionally until it is smooth and making sure it doesn't burn.

When the jelly is melted, add the vinegar and stir to combine. Add the red pepper flakes, if using, and salt and stir again. If the glaze is too thick, add a bit more vinegar. Mix and taste. Adjust seasoning if necessary.

You can use warm or let cool and transfer to clean glass jars. The glaze will keep covered in the refrigerator for up to 1 week.

Fire-Roasted Vodka Sauce

Makes about 6 cups; save any extra for pasta

1   tablespoon extra-virgin olive oil

1   tablespoon unsalted butter

2   cloves garlic, minced

2   shallots, minced

1½ cans fire-roasted tomatoes (48 ounces)

½   cup vodka

Coarse salt and white pepper

Pinch of chile flakes

½   cup heavy cream

Fresh basil, whole or julienne

Heat a large skillet over medium. Add the oil, butter, garlic, and shallots. Gently sauté the shallots for 3 to 5 minutes to develop their sweetness. Add the tomatoes, then the vodka, and cook for 2 to 3 minutes.

Bring the sauce to a boil, then reduce the heat to simmer. Season with salt, pepper, and chile flakes. Purée with an immersion blender or transfer to a regular blender.

Stir the cream into the sauce and heat through; season with basil.

Autumn Cranberry Chutney

Serves 8

	Juice and zest of a large orange (about ½ cup of juice)
1	tablespoon balsamic vinegar
1	cup port
1	cup filtered water
1	cup sugar
2	12-ounce bags of fresh or frozen cranberries
1	cup whole dried Turkish apricots, cut into slivers
1	cup dried cherries
	Pinch of kosher salt
¼	teaspoon nutmeg
¼	teaspoon ground clove
1	teaspoon ground cinnamon

In a large, heavy-bottomed pot, add the juice and zest of the orange, the balsamic vinegar, port, water, sugar, and cranberries. Bring to a simmer and add the dried fruit, a pinch of salt, the nutmeg, clove, and cinnamon. Cook until the cranberries start to pop, stirring occasionally, about 15 to 20 minutes. Taste and adjust the seasonings if necessary.

Cassis Sauce

Makes about 1 cup

1	tablespoon olive oil
2	shallots, diced finely
2	tablespoons balsamic vinegar
1	cup unsweetened black currant jam, black cherry, or similar preserve, divided
2	tablespoons crème de cassis
	Freshly ground black pepper

Heat a heavy pan over medium-high heat. When hot, add the oil and shallots. Stir occasionally for 3 minutes, or until the shallots begin to turn golden.

Remove from the heat, add the vinegar to the pan, and stir with a wooden spoon. Add the jam, crème de cassis, and black pepper.

Return to the heat and stir occasionally for 3 minutes.

Southern Sausage Dressing

Makes 8 to 10 cups

1   large package Pepperidge Farm® herb-seasoned stuffing or gluten-free savory stuffing mix

8   slices favorite bread or gluten-free bread, crumbled

1   pound bulk hot pork sage sausage (preferably Neese's® brand)

1   bunch celery, chopped

2   yellow onions, chopped

1   stick butter, melted

1   can (15 ounces) low-salt no-fat chicken broth, or 15 ounces homemade stock

    Kosher salt and freshly ground black pepper

In a large bowl, mix together the package of stuffing mix and the fresh breadcrumbs and set aside, tossing occasionally so the crumbs dry out. Meanwhile, cook the sausage in a medium skillet until it's completely cooked through; remove with a slotted spoon and drain on paper towels. Remove and discard all but 2 tablespoons of the pork fat.

In the same skillet, sauté the celery and onions until they're soft and the onions begin to caramelize, 7 to 10 minutes. Mix the vegetables, sausage, and melted butter with the breadcrumbs until well combined. Moisten with the chicken broth until the stuffing holds together but is not too wet. Season with salt and pepper.

Place the stuffing in a buttered 9x13x2 casserole dish and bake at 350°F for 35 to 40 minutes or until the top is browned. (Alternatively, you can stuff the turkey just before cooking but this will make it "stuffing." "Dressing" is the preferred lingo in the South and it is always on the side!)

Pan Gravy

Makes about 1 cup

	Giblets and neck bone from turkey
2	celery ribs with leaves, cut into 2-inch pieces
1	small onion, cut into eighths
	Drippings from the turkey roast pan
¼	cup unbleached all-purpose flour or gluten-free flour + extra if needed
½	cup white wine (optional)
	Kosher salt and freshly ground black pepper to taste

Place the giblets, neck bone, celery, and onions in a saucepan with 2 cups of water. Let simmer for 1½ hours. Strain and retain the liquid, discarding the vegetables, neck, and giblets; set aside. Heat the turkey pan drippings in a sauté pan over medium heat; add a little of the reserved giblet liquid and the flour and whisk for 3 to 5 minutes until the flour is browned (this eliminates the raw flour taste). Stir in the wine (if using) and a little more of the reserved giblet liquid until the consistency is smooth and thick. Adjust the seasonings and serve with smashed potatoes, Southern Sausage Dressing, and turkey.

Hot Pepper Jelly

Makes 5½ cups; jar the rest and give as hostess gifts

½	cup chopped green bell peppers
¾	cups chopped red bell peppers
¼	cup chopped jalapeños (2 to 3 seeded and stemmed)
1½	cups cider vinegar
6½	cups sugar
6	ounces pectin
2	teaspoons crushed red chile flakes

Put the bell and jalapeño peppers and vinegar in a food processor or blender and purée. Pour the purée into a large pot and add the sugar. Bring to a boil and boil for 3 minutes.

Whisk in the pectin and continue boiling for 1 minute, then skim the foam from the top. Remove the pan from the heat and let sit 5 for minutes; skim any foam again. Stir in the red chile flakes.

Pour the hot pepper jelly into hot sterilized jelly jars. Seal and store in cool place.

Note: Store the jelly in sterilized jars. I sterilize my jars in the dishwasher and time it so the cycle is finished when the jelly is done. If you've never sterilized jars, check the procedure online or in books about canning and preserving.

B&E Drizzle-icious Infused Oil

This oil is a fabulous finishing touch on any freshly cooked pizza.

Makes 15 ounces

1	16-ounce bottle good-quality extra-virgin olive oil
5	cloves garlic, slightly crushed
3	dried red chile peppers
	Zest of 1 orange, removed with a vegetable peeler (use outer orange layer of peel only)
3	sprigs fresh rosemary
1	tablespoon multicolor peppercorns

Pour out 3 tablespoons of the oil and stuff the other ingredients into the bottle. Seal and refrigerate for a minimum of 2 days before using. Always keep refrigerated to avoid spoilage by the garlic.

This will keep, tightly capped, for up to a month.

B&E Sprinkle-icious Spice Blend

Enhance any pizza, salad, or flatbread with a shake or two.

Makes ½ cup

1	tablespoon dehydrated onion
1	tablespoon roasted dehydrated garlic
2	teaspoons dried lemon peel
½	teaspoon red pepper flakes
1	teaspoon dried thyme
2	tablespoons kosher salt
2	teaspoons freshly ground black pepper

Mix all the ingredients thoroughly and store in an airtight container for up to 3 months.

Red Wine–Poached Figs

Makes about 1½ cups

18 dried figs (packaged in a ring)

1½ cups hearty red wine

3 ounces cognac (optional)

1 cup firmly packed dark brown sugar

   Zest from 1 lemon, finely grated with a Microplane or zester

1 cinnamon stick

Stem the figs and cut in half. Place in a medium saucepan and add the wine, cognac, brown sugar, lemon zest, and cinnamon stick. Bring to a boil, reduce the heat to a medium-low, and simmer for 5 minutes. Remove from the heat, cover, and let cool in the poaching liquid.

When the figs are cool, remove from the liquid. If preparing in advance, keep them stored in the liquid.

These will keep, tightly covered, in the refrigerator for up to 3 days.

How to Supreme Citrus Fruit

To supreme any citrus fruit (oranges, grapefruit, etc.), begin by cutting ¼ inch off each end. Then stand the fruit up on one end and slice off all the skin along with the outer membrane of the sections (thereby exposing the flesh). Holding the fruit in the palm of your hand, use your knife to cut inside the membrane of each individual segment. This will produce individual segments.

How to Toast Nuts

Preheat the oven to 300°F. Spread the nuts on a baking sheet in a single layer and bake until golden brown, 5 to 15 minutes, depending on the nut variety. Turn once during cooking. Let cool before using.

How to Toast Coconut

Preheat the oven to 300°F. Spread the grated coconut on a baking sheet in a single layer and bake until golden brown, about 7 minutes, depending on the thickness of the shred. Turn once during cooking. Let cool before using. Note: Sweetened coconut will brown quicker because of the sugar content.

Metric Equivalents

LIQUID/DRY MEASURES	
U.S.	METRIC
¼ teaspoon	1.25 milliliters
½ teaspoon	2.5 milliliters
1 teaspoon	5 milliliters
1 tablespoon (3 teaspoons)	15 milliliters
1 fluid ounce (2 tablespoons)	30 milliliters
¼ cup	60 milliliters
⅓ cup	80 milliliters
½ cup	120 milliliters
1 cup	240 milliliters
1 pint (2 cups)	480 milliliters
1 quart (4 cups; 32 ounces)	960 milliliters
1 gallon (4 quarts)	3.84 liters
1 ounce (by weight)	28 grams
1 pound	454 grams
2.2 pounds	1 kilogram

OVEN TEMPERATURES		
°F	GAS MARK	°C
250	½	120
275	1	140
300	2	150
325	3	165
350	4	180
375	5	190
400	6	200
425	7	220
450	8	230
475	9	240
500	10	260
550	Broil	290

INDEX

Numbers in **bold** indicate pages with photographs

ELIZABETH KARMEL is the author of *Soaked, Slathered, and Seasoned* and *Taming the Flame,* writes a column for Associated Press, and is the executive chef of Hill Country Barbecue Market and Country Chicken (locations in New York City, Brooklyn, and Washington, D.C.) She is the creator of www.GrillsattheGrill.com and Elizabeth Karmel's GrillFriends, a line of kitchen and grilling tools.

BOB BLUMER is the creator and host of the award-winning Food Network shows *Surreal Gourmet* and *Glutton for Punishment,* and the host of *World's Weirdest Restaurants.* He holds seven food-related Guinness World Records and is the author of five cookbooks, most recently *Glutton for Pleasure.*